THE NEXT GENERATION OF ROCK & PUNK

NU-METAL

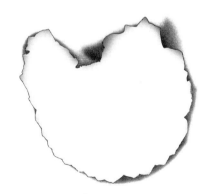

THE NEXT GENERATION OF ROCK & PUNK

NU-METAL

JOEL McIVER

OMNIBUS PRESS

Cover & book designed by Phil Gambrill.
Picture research by Nikki Lloyd.

ISBN: 0.7119.9209-6
Order No: OP48873

EXCLUSIVE DISTRIBUTORS
Music Sales Limited,
8/9 Frith Street, London W1D 3JB, UK.

Music Sales Corporation,
257 Park Avenue South, New York, NY 10010, USA.

Macmillan Distribution Services,
53 Park West Drive, Derrimut, Vic 3030, Australia.

TO THE MUSIC TRADE ONLY:
Music Sales Limited,
8/9 Frith Street, London W1D 3JB, UK.

Photo credits: J. Athill: 47; Richard Beland/SIN: 94;
George Chin/Redferns: 46; Nigel Crane: 127;
Grant Davis/Redferns: 2, 75l;
George Desota/Redferns: 68; Isabella De Wit: 143;
Steve Double/SIN: 105; courtesy of Fake: 52;
Fotex/Stefan Malzorn/Redferns: 102;
courtesy of Future Management: 31; Mick
Hutson/Redferns: 29, 36, 39, 51, 80, 89;
Martin Jeffery: 112, 119; LFI: front & back cover,
8, 11, 15, 16, 18, 19, 21, 22, 25, 26, 28, 32, 33, 34,
35, 40, 41, 45, 48, 49, 53, 54, 55, 56, 57, 58,
59, 60, 61, 63, 66, 67, 69, 70, 72, 73, 75r, 76,
79, 81, 83, 84b, 87, 90, 91, 92, 93, 96, 97, 98,
99, 101, 103, 108, 111, 113, 116, 118, 122,
124, 125, 126, 129, 131, 132, 136, 137, 139, 141;
Anthony Medley/SIN: 64; Courtesy of
Mercury Rain: 82; Tony Mott/SIN: back cover,
42, 115; Marcus O'Higgins: 84t; Doralba
Picerno/SIN: 6, 62, 88; Alessio Pitticannella/
SIN: 121, 135; Courtesy of Susan Rand
Management: 110; Ebet Roberts/Redferns: 104;
Annie Sumanska-Fulcher: 30; Roy Tee/SIN: 95;
Vincenzo Turello/courtesy of Earache: 78;
Greg Waterman: 23; Andy Willsher/SIN: 27,107.

www.omnibuspress.com

ACKNOWLEDGMENTS

Compiling a book such as this is only
possible with a lot of help. These are the
people without whose unselfish assistance
this volume could not exist. In other words,
it's all their fault, so blame them.

Michelle Kerr and Alison Edwards
(Roadrunner), Kas Mercer and Lisa McNamee
(Mercenary PR), Karl Demata (Plastic Head),
Roland Hyams, Nik Moore and
Petrina MacFarlane (Work Hard PR),
Gary Levermore (Noise), Sarah Lees (Earache),
Sarah Watson (Virgin)

The tireless *Record Collector* staff:
Andy, Daryl, Tim, Jack and Jake –
quite frankly, it's a good scene!

The loyal warriors of metal I've met
since deciding in a moment of madness
to start writing books on the subject:
Tom Squire, Bruce Zombie, Paul Stenning,
Sam Dunn, Joe Ambrose, Quinn Harrington,
Cristiano Mastrangeli, Giuliano D'Amico,
Greg Moffitt, Ian Glasper, Ross Hicks,
Ryan Downey, Brady Brock, Jamie Stead,
Daniel Brand, Sean Plummer, Martin Popoff,
Kyle Munson, Matthew Colontrelle,
Dan Lorenzo, Chris Turton

Many thanks to Casey Chaos for his
eloquent foreword.

Unlimited respect to Robin, Dad,
John & Jen, Woody & Glynis, Lucy & Johnny,
Dave, Phil & Kate, David & Arline, Matt,
the Bossmann-Everitt dynasty and everyone
else who tolerates me ranting on about
Slipknot all the time.

Most of all, love to my beautiful wife, Emma.

Got a comment about this book?
Mail me personally at joel@joelmciver.co.uk
C'mon, I can take it . . .

JOEL McIVER, OCTOBER 2001

This book is dedicated to Jean Whittle.

Oi!

Welcome to **NU-METAL: The Next Generation Of Rock And Punk**, an autopsy
of modern music. The atrocities of sound can change lives and shift the axis of this
world through money or passion. It will be heard and packaged for you to consume.
Music or commodity? It's your decision, alone in your room discovering your
own bands, creating your own personal soundtrack to live your life by and feel like
your first orgasm.

Music is food for the soul. You got fast-food music designed for the masses to get
fat and rich. Then you have extreme music, underground music that has always set
the trends for fashion, art, language and film. It is the most powerful medium there
is, and has always set the standard for future generations to police and buy what is
pure, and annihilate the listener with the truth. What they never told you in history
class is what they don't play on the radio. It is the fear of change, and the strength
of commodity. Are you accountable and/or responsible for their sins of capitalism?
You decide.

Check out The Stooges, Black Flag, Discharge, Slayer, Fugazi, The Damned,
Einstürzende Neubauten, Necrophagia, Void, Swans, Queens Of The Stone Age,
Diamanda Galas, Birthday Party, or The Ramones and hear the influence they have
spread across this wretched land. I've had the pleasure of meeting a lot of the people
I grew up listening to, and I've found these humans are just as real as their bands
and the music they created. From Iggy Pop to Rat Scabies to Rikk Agnew, to Josh
and Nick to Omar and Cedric to Kurt and Grohl, to Brian May to Lydia Lunch,
there's no phony rock star shit, and it's apparent in their sound as well. Any good
music creates a reaction; love it or hate it. Indifference is a tool of the sleeping.

I'm not really sure why Joel asked me to write this foreword. Probably to show
that if I can do this, anyone can. So, the same rules apply: Go start your own band.
Do it yourself. Long live the sound of bands in their garage.

Refuse Amen.

An American Wanker,

Casey Chaos of Amen

MUDVAYNE

THE SHOCK OF THE NEW

NOT SURE ABOUT THIS NU-METAL MALARKEY?
CONFUSED BETWEEN OLD AND NEW, EXTREME AND MAINSTREAM?
THEN READ ON FOR INSTANT ENLIGHTENMENT!

JUST WHAT THE HELL IS 'NU-METAL', ANYWAY?

It's the modern form of heavy metal, which has been in existence since the early Seventies. Nu-metal is less constrained to a single sound and image than the original version and addresses wider issues, too. Think about 'new metal' as opposed to 'old metal' and you're most of the way there - 'nu' or 'new', the meaning is the same. But it's not the name that matters - it's all about the way it sounds. Listening to the music for a few minutes will tell you more about it than any label ever will.

WHO INVENTED THE TERM 'NU-METAL'?

No idea – probably a music journalist in the mid-Nineties. You might also have heard of the terms 'rap-metal', 'rap-rock', 'rapcore', and so on. These are all rapidly becoming obsolete, because the music is about much more than rapping - although that's certainly how it started. 'Emo-metal', 'emo-core' or simply 'emo' are also common terms - referring to the often emotional lyrics of modern metal bands - but again, these terms are of limited value. 'Nu-metal' is a broad enough label to cover the whole scene, although some pundits argue that it too has more specific connotations.

However, any band will tell you that categorisation is pointless - and that's the approach to take. Don't get too hung up on the labels: focus on the music. For our purposes, if it's modern metal and it derives a certain proportion of its sound from hip-hop, punk, glam rock or funk, it's in.

HOW DID WE GET TO NU-METAL FROM OLD METAL?

This is the key question, and one that is impossible to answer briefly. Perhaps more than any style of music, heavy metal has had to reinvent itself completely in the last decade. The journey from old to new has been long and tortuous...

We can start by casting our minds back to **grunge**. Just as most of the progressive rock dinosaurs of the Seventies were subverted and ultimately wiped out by the unwashed legions of punk, heavy metal – an apparently healthy, flourishing art form – was overwhelmed by the plaid-shirted hordes of grunge bands that emerged from the Seattle backwoods in the wake of one seminal album: Nirvana's 1991 masterpiece, *Nevermind*. In the space of a single year, it seemed that metal was old hat and grunge was where popular music was going.

Only the most talented, adaptable or downright eccentric heavy metal bands survived this formidable sea-change to emerge, bruised and humbled, when the tide of grunge finally receded after Nirvana singer Kurt Cobain's suicide in April 1994. This streamlining of heavy metal is now widely thought to have been A Good Thing: metal had run wild in the Eighties and there were far too many Guns N'Roses hair-metal clones around – pompous, preening acts with better make-up and backcombing skills than songwriting. Admit it - Poison, Warrant, Ratt, Cinderella and their cheesy LA colleagues weren't supposed to survive the Eighties, were they?

After grunge, which made angst-ridden lyrics and organic, sludgy production techniques *de rigueur*, only the best, most forward-thinking metal bands could attract many listeners: a prime example of survival of the fittest, as it were.

But the roots of nu-metal can be traced back further than grunge. The first form of nu-metal (for our purposes, heavy music that tried to be more intelligent and versatile than simple yelled vocals over riffs and percussion) was **rap-metal**, which started – as you might imagine – when someone rapped over an overdriven guitar for the first time.

The first successful example of a rap-metal tune came in September 1986 (exactly fifteen years before the completion of this book), when Run DMC and Aerosmith collaborated on a reworked version of the latter's classic 'Walk This Way' and topped the singles charts worldwide. Five months later came the Beastie Boys,

The self-styled Antichrist Superstar, MARILYN MANSON

who released several singles including the puerile but influential '(You Gotta) Fight For Your Right (To Party)', which featured guitar riffs by Kerry King of Slayer. This was followed up by US homeboy Tone Loc, whose February 1989 hit 'Wild Thing' contained a simple riff under Loc's famously laconic rap. Other early rap-metal milestones were Faith No More's 'Epic' in February 1990 and 'Bring The Noise' by Chuck D and Anthrax in July 1991. The rap-metal floodgates subsequently opened to allow dozens of rappin' rockers out of the woodwork, and the movement was born.

A less successful and less prominent sub-genre was **funk-metal**, a slightly clumsy term applied in the late Eighties to any rock band whose bass player used a slapping style: the best-known funk-metallers were The Red Hot Chili Peppers (who later achieved global success with a more pop-oriented approach) and Living Colour (an impossibly talented group of players who were just too far ahead of their time to keep it together for long). Other funk-metallers ranged from the credible, such as Infectious Grooves (a side-project of hardcore punks Suicidal Tendencies), to the abysmal, with The Dan Reed Network a best-forgotten example.

When these new styles joined forces with grunge against the traditional metal bands, even mainstream rock acts such as The Cult were unable to sustain much impetus. For a metal band to survive, it had to be diverse (Faith No More, Primus), too big to touch (Metallica, Iron Maiden) or too small to count (the vast underground legions of black and death metal bands). Even apparent untouchables such as Motörhead and Mötley Crüe survived only by the skin of their teeth.

By the early to mid-Nineties, the new style was king. Rage Against The Machine emerged from Los Angeles in 1993, taking rap and rock to new levels with their self-titled debut album, and the following year another Californian act, Korn, became the first band to be labelled a 'nu-metal' act. The rest is history. But it's a very *recent* history – and this is the first book to attempt to catalogue the movement. You'll find pioneers of the style such as the two mentioned above in these pages, as well as the very newest of the new breed, which means that three decades (the Eighties, Nineties and Noughties) are covered by this book.

HOW IS NU-METAL DIFFERENT FROM OLD METAL?

The sound, lyrics and image of nu-metal all distinguish it from the old school. Musically, it's more diverse, with influences taken from a variety of fields:

HIP-HOP. The most obvious import. Traditional heavy metal bands would have shuddered at the mere thought of using drum machines, samples, rapping and scratching in their songs, but these are a mainstay of dozens of bands in this book, a notable example being Limp Bizkit.

ELECTRONICA. Broadly, this means keyboard or computer-sourced sounds which are harsher or have less groove than hip-hop. This can mean mellow ambient sounds, or a cortex-shredding barrage of white noise (see Atari Teenage Riot or Pitchshifter).

FUNK. The sweaty, sexual grind of this vintage genre permeates the work of many a nu-metal outfit, most prominently Korn. This is what transforms metal from music for moshers into music for dancers, baby.

HARDCORE PUNK. Fast, gritty, murkily-produced: the grimiest music of them all is welcome at the altar of nu-metal - see Amen, Stampin' Ground and many others.

JAZZ. The gently atonal chords, noodling solos and unpredictable chord sequences of the old idiom often crop up in the work of more dexterous, progressive bands such as Tool and the early Slipknot.

INDUSTRIAL ROCK. A common source of inspiration. The grinding samples, military beats, harsh textures and intimidating images of industrial may not be for everyone, although followers of Rammstein, Nine Inch Nails and the others would probably disagree strongly.

GOTHIC ROCK. Blame The Sisters Of Mercy: their gloomy, ice-cold sounds, grim shades-and-black-garb look and dabbling with horror and pagan themes form the obvious template for Coal Chamber, Orgy and a whole host of professional miserablists.

GLAM ROCK.
Two words: Marilyn Manson.

While nu-metal is still guitar-based (it's still metal, after all, with all that genre's earth-shaking, parent-displeasing connotations), the turntable, the sequencer and the sampler are almost as integral to the sound as the old-fashioned axe. The guitar itself is often a seven-string and may also be downtuned for the sake of heaviness, forcing bass players to adopt five- and six-string instruments.

Lyrically, it's more open than the metal of before: if it's macho, it's being ironic. Think back to the time-honoured themes of heavy metal: it was the old school's job to sing about war, motorbikes, shagging, Satanism, wizards and dragons, and life on the road (which often featured all the previous elements). There's little of this in nu-metal. Frontmen such as Jonathan Davis of Korn, and later Amen's Casey Chaos and Slipknot's Corey Taylor, have made it acceptable (cynics have often said 'fashionable') to reveal their deepest hurt in their lyrics.

There's also a willingness to explore serious (and even taboo) subjects in nu-metal which was almost entirely lacking in the old days. Old-style anthems such as Iron Maiden's 'Women In Uniform', Judas Priest's 'Breaking The Law' or AC/DC's 'Ballbreaker' – great as these old songs undoubtedly are - were hardly paeans to depression, domestic abuse and existential anxiety, all of which are themes explored in nu-metal. The hard men of rock have, it seems, examined their inner selves, and found them wanting.

Visually, the new style is still recognisable as metal – fans and bands alike still wear T-shirts, tattoos and studs – but short hair is as common as long, piercings and make-up are often the norm and combat/hip-hop wear is more acceptable than the standard denim and leather of the old school. At last, metal is cool: your Eighties metaller, long mocked for his greasy locks, skin-tight jeans and unwashed T-shirt, has been forced underground – but make no mistake, he'll be back when the wheel of fashion completes its next turn.

In essence, then, nu metal is more multifaceted, more accepting and much more self-aware than the old style, which had to change due to musical trends in order to survive.

IS NU-METAL COMMERCIALLY SUCCESSFUL?

Just a bit. It's the most popular music in the world at the time of writing. Either today's music fans have come to metal, or the music has come to them – it's hard to say which, and it probably doesn't matter. Having reached its commercial peak in the Seventies, old-school heavy metal remained a niche market through the Eighties, with little radio airplay and hardly any chart presence. But the Nineties saw a redoubled demand for hard music, and in the first years of the new century, metal has a fanbase in every country that plays music.

At the same time, of course, mainstream pop is bigger, blander and more nauseating than ever before (look at the sales clout of saccharine-drenched teen acts such as Britney Spears, Westlife and The Backstreet Boys) but the flipside of this is that you can now hear metal on TV or commercial radio, which you couldn't have done ten years ago.

Predictably, the record companies have noticed that their customers want more metal and have responded to this demand by a) employing metal-aware A&R and marketing staff and b) embarking on a promotional spending spree. Like everything else which is popular, there's money to be made out of metal.

Culturally, economically and musically, society has become more 'metal', which will please, depress, irritate or delight you, depending entirely on your point of view.

WHO ARE THE TOP NU-METAL BANDS?

At the time of writing (mid-2001) it's possible to identify a Big Three Of Nu-Metal, just as there was a Big Four Of Thrash (Metallica, Megadeth, Anthrax and Slayer) in the Eighties. In terms of selling power (biggest first), these are currently **Limp Bizkit**, **Korn** and **Slipknot**, all of which have received extended entries in this guide by virtue of their massive drawing-power as a live act and their pioneering status. It's hard to say if these three will still be holding sway in a couple of years' time, but currently they all enjoy vast critical and commercial success and show no signs of slowing down. Contenders for the throne are currently **Tool**, **Amen** and **Deftones** – but it only takes one big hit to change things completely, and new acts are emerging all the time.

Below these A and B leagues are bands such as **Fear Factory**, **Papa Roach**, **Linkin Park**, **Disturbed**, **Soulfly**, **Queens Of The Stone Age**, **Raging Speedhorn** and **System Of A Down**, all of which plough very different musical furrows but can still be grouped under the eclectic nu-metal banner. And then, one step further down, there are literally hundreds of other acts. Over 100 of these appear in this book: a volume containing every likely-looking nu-metal outfit that exists would be five times bigger than the one you're holding, and my hair would have gone grey. So don't complain.

Somewhat to one side of all these bands stands the remarkable **Marilyn Manson**, whose nu-metal influences are clear. But this group is as much a rock or a glam band as a metal act, and as such is something of an interesting oddity. Similarly, there is **Nine Inch Nails**, whose career started before the nu-metal trend had taken off but whose industrial-metal combination was undoubtedly an enormous influence on the whole movement. Whether these two bands fall within the confines of nu-metal is open to debate: the same goes for many of the more punk, hip-hop or gothic outfits to be found in these pages.

But all the bands here are both metallic and non-traditional in style, and so they qualify. Another point to bear in mind is that most of the biggest bands are American: it will take some time for other countries to provide serious contenders, although you'll find dozens of excellent British and European bands in this book who have a good chance of toppling the throne.

If you insist on a Top 20 of nu-metal, here it is: the list below is an estimation of the world's biggest bands of this style (and before anyone gets pedantic, placings take into account overall media presence and industry influence, not just record sales):

01 LIMP BIZKIT
02 SLIPKNOT
03 KORN
04 TOOL
05 MARILYN MANSON
06 SOULFLY
07 DEFTONES
08 FEAR FACTORY
09 AMEN
10 QUEENS OF THE STONE AGE
11 NINE INCH NAILS
12 PAPA ROACH
13 COAL CHAMBER
14 LINKIN PARK
15 SYSTEM OF A DOWN
16 STAIND
17 SPINESHANK
18 RAGING SPEEDHORN
19 PAYABLE ON DEATH
20 GLASSJAW

This is merely a snapshot of the current situation at the time of writing. As I mentioned before, one successful release can alter the balance completely, so don't take this as some form of unholy gospel. Having said that, the Top 10 of this list has been pretty much as it appears above for the last couple of years.

WHAT'S THE FUTURE OF NU-METAL?

The good thing about nu-metal is its diversity. While the actual term 'nu-metal' must inevitably fall out of fashion, the music it represents will not simply die out. Metal will always be with us in some form or other – with or without its current trademark keyboards, DJs, effects, therapy-based lyrics and hip-hop beats. The nu-metal incarnation is simply the most versatile version yet to emerge.

People want cathartic music, and no musical form provides a more violent catharsis than metal. It's not for everyone, of course – it's not supposed to be. But for those who want it, metal will always be there in some form or other. Just accept it.

The chocolate starfish himself:
Fred Durst of LIMP BIZKIT

IT'S THEIR FAULT...

THE PEOPLE WHO MADE IT HAPPEN

Nu-metal is a relatively young genre, and as such has been shaped by a small number of influential individuals, companies and events. Throughout the 140 or so entries which make up this guide you'll come across the same names on several occasions – so here's a quick bluffer's guide to the handful of pioneers that made it happen, including five seminal bands, a producer, a record company and an annual metal tour. After all, they're the reason you're reading this book.

Read this section carefully – and if someone comes up to you at a party and says, "Hey, did you see that Ross Robinson's new band, Dismembered Badger 777, has just signed a deal with Roadrunner and is playing at next year's Ozzfest? Apparently they sound like classic FNM, Chilis and Beasties, with elements of Jane's Addiction and Nirvana. Do you want to go and see them?" then you'll know exactly what to say...

FAITH NO MORE

THE BAND THAT STARTED IT ALL
WHO WERE THEY?

A San Francisco Bay area band consisting initially of bassist Billy Gould, drummer Mike 'Puffy' Bordin, keyboard player Wade Worthington and guitarist Mark Bowen, Faith No More started life in 1981 as Faith No Man. Recruiting various temporary singers including future Hole frontwoman Courtney Love, the band ended up with Chuck Mosely, and the line-up settled down when Bowen was replaced by Jim Martin. Worthington was also replaced by the bizarrely-named Roddy Bottum, and the band changed its name to Faith No More.

A four-song demo led to a deal with the independent Mordam label and an album, *We Care A Lot*, appeared in 1985. The title track combined Gould's percussive bass with the heavy riffs of Martin, and can be seen with hindsight as one of the very first funk-metal songs.

FNM then moved to another record company, Slash, which released *Introduce Yourself* in 1987. Epic ballads such as 'Anne's Song' and mellow strumathons such as 'The Crab Song' combined with the harder material to make it a bona fide classic. A world tour followed, but Mosely had fallen out with the other musicians and

FAITH NO MORE: the late, great rap-metal pioneers

was ousted when the band got home in January 1989.

The crucial move that propelled FNM to stardom came when vocalist Mike Patton, of the Californian band Mr. Bungle, took Mosely's place. A freakishly animated performer with considerable vision, Patton took the band by the scruff of the neck and inspired them to far greater efforts. The resulting album, *The Real Thing*, was an absolute landmark, with driving riffs aplenty courtesy of the eccentric Martin, Patton's spiralling harmonies and sinister whispers and the expert textures of Gould, Bottum and Bordin making it an eye-opener for fans unused to this new, varied approach to metal.

A tour with metal giants Metallica pushed Faith No More further into the public eye: this was compounded by the enormous success of the song 'Epic', released in early 1990. A Grammy nomination and the public support of leading rockers such as Guns N'Roses' Axl Rose followed.

Mainstream success – once unimaginable for this quirkiest of bands – was achieved in 1991 and 1992 thanks to a live video, *You Fat Bastards* (no, I'm not making this up), a live recording and the hugely popular fourth album, *Angel Dust*. The record marked the peak of FNM's fortunes and stayed near the top of the charts for months, helped along by the excellent singles 'Midlife Crisis', 'A Small Victory' and a cover of the Commodores' 'Easy', a surprise No. 1 which led to a reissue of *Angel Dust*.

However, the rot was setting in a little and the increasingly demotivated Jim Martin departed in November 1993. He was replaced by Mr. Bungle axeman Trey Spruance on the next album, 1995's *King For A Day, Fool For A Lifetime*, but the moment had passed and the album didn't sell well outside the FNM hardcore fanbase. Spruance himself didn't last long and his place was taken by Duh guitarist Dean Menta.

Solo projects from Bottum (Imperial Teen) and Patton (Mr. Bungle and solo albums) followed, and 1997's coyly-titled *Album Of The Year* proved to be Faith No More's last. In April 1998 Gould released the following message: "After 15 long and fruitful years, Faith No More have decided to put an end to speculation regarding their imminent break-up... by breaking up.

The decision among the members is mutual, and there will be no pointing of fingers, no naming of names, other than stating, for the record, that 'Puffy started it'. Furthermore, the split will now enable each member to pursue his individual project(s) unhindered. Lastly, and most importantly, the band would like to thank all of those fans and associates that have stuck with and supported the band throughout its history."

The fans were dismayed, but accepted that although Faith No More's pioneering status was evident, their relevance in the era of nu-metal was questionable. Patton has gone on to form Fantomas and Tomahawk and launch a record label, Ipecac, while the others are still making music in some capacity or other.

HOW DID FAITH NO MORE INFLUENCE NU-METAL?

They were the first of the Eighties funk-metal bands to make an impact and opened thousands of fans' eyes to the fact that heavy metal need not confine itself to hair-metal anthems or extreme metal brutality. They deserve the maximum respect of anyone who has ever enjoyed a heavy riff in the Nineties and beyond.

WHY SHOULD WE CARE ABOUT FAITH NO MORE?

Because they were pioneers, and way, way ahead of their time.

RED HOT CHILI PEPPERS

TAKING FUNK-METAL TO THE MASSES

WHO ARE THEY?

The Red Hot Chili Peppers are perceived by most rock fans nowadays as a pleasant chart act without much of particular consequence to offer. This is due to their recent promotion to the vanguard of alternative rock and, it must be said, to a degree of over-exposure. However, back in the mid-Eighties the band were an entirely different proposition – raw, sexual and unrefined, their potent brand of funk-metal was fast, powerful and unpredictable, placing them second only to Faith No More in the pioneering stakes.

Founded by the phenomenal bass player Michael Balzary (aka Flea) and singer

Anthony Kiedis in the early Eighties in Los Angeles, the Chilis fused their punk roots (courtesy of guitarist Hillel Slovak) with metal (drummer Jack Irons was a long-established headbanger) and funk, the latter courtesy of the frighteningly nimble-fingered Flea. Three early albums, *Red Hot Chili Peppers* (1984), *Freaky Styley* (1985), *The Uplift Mofo Party Plan* (1987) and an EP, *Abbey Road* (1988, featuring the band strolling naked across the famous London zebra crossing) gained the band a cult following without unduly troubling the charts.

The line-up was soon hit by tragedy, however, when Slovak succumbed to a heroin overdose in 1988. Irons duly left, unable to continue, and the band fell silent for a time. Kiedis and Flea then returned with new guitarist John Frusciante and drummer Chad Smith and the Chili Peppers' first significant success came with the release of *Mother's Milk* the following year, a multifaceted album featuring the anthemic 'Higher Ground'.

Hardcore Peppers fans were still trying to come to terms with the fact that their favourite underground act had become a radio favourite (followers of Metallica and Faith No More were in the same unlikely situation at the time) when the band took another giant step forward with their global smash, *Blood Sugar Sex Magik*. Produced by the mega-bearded super-producer Rick Rubin, the album boasted a crisp, accessible sound and rapidly sold over two million copies, thanks to the singles 'Under The Bridge', a heartfelt, anthemic ballad, and 'Give It Away', a slab of pure funk nailed to Flea's simple but killer bass riff.

In 1992 Frusciante left the band and spent a couple of years in drug hell. His replacements included Arik Marshall, Jesse Tobias and sometime Jane's Addiction guitarist Dave Navarro, who added a certain quirky panache to 1995's *One Hot Minute*. This eagerly-awaited album failed, however, to deliver the commercial impact of its predecessor. An exhausting world tour ensued, with Flea occasionally taking time out to guest with a variety of other bands (he and Navarro backed Alanis Morissette on her vengeful 'You Oughta Know' single, for example), which allowed the Chilis to consolidate their position in the global Top 10 of rock.

RED HOT CHILI PEPPERS:
Nobody weird like them

Navarro subsequently quit after deciding that life on the road was not for him. The move turned out to be beneficial for the group, who re-recruited the now-clean John Frusciante in 1998 and invested the next album, 1999's *Californication*, with a new enthusiasm. The Red Hot Chili Peppers remain at the top of the rock tree, having earned undying respect for their work – except from the original underground fans, of course, many of whom regard their enormous success as a sell-out. But that's often the way it goes.

HOW DID THEY INFLUENCE NU-METAL?

By bringing 'the funk' to metal in an intelligent way, this remarkable band changed the face of rock. They've also demonstrated that ballads have their place in metal, and that previously dodgy themes (drug addiction, unrequited love) can be addressed in a meaningful way – even if you're a headbanger.

WHY SHOULD WE CARE ABOUT THE RED HOT CHILI PEPPERS?

Because if they didn't exist, it would be necessary to invent them.

BEASTIE BOYS

SILLY, SOPHISTICATED AND SUCCESSFUL

WHO ARE THEY?

Simply the first white band to pilfer the sound of black funk and hip-hop and turn it into globally successful rock. Like Vanilla Ice, Eminem and a host of white-boy rappers in the Nineties and Noughties, the fact that the Beastie Boys were Caucasian meant that aficionados were initially unconvinced of their abilities. Add to this the band-members' wealthy backgrounds, and it's little wonder that few listeners took them seriously on an early appearance in 1983, when they abandoned their hardcore punk roots on a comedy rap single, 'Cookie Puss'.

Ironically, as a punk band the Beastie Boys had enjoyed much more credibility. Initially consisting of vocalist Mike D (Michael Diamond), guitarist John Berry, bassist MCA (Adam Yauch) and drummer Kate Schellenbach (later to return in the band Luscious Jackson), the band had formed in Manhattan in 1981.

Demonstrating their Black Flag influences on the *Pollywog Stew* EP, released by the local Ratcage label, the group scored support slots with The Misfits but were hampered by the early departure of Berry and Schellenbach.

The move to a rap direction came after the recruitment of Ad-Rock (Adam Horovitz, the son of playwright Israel Horovitz). After the 'Cookie Puss' single became a surprise club hit, the trio hooked up with the New York student Rick Rubin (see Red Hot Chili Peppers, above), who was looking for bands to sign to his new label, Def Jam. A second single, the feebly-titled 'Rock Hard', failed to cut the proverbial mustard, but the follow-up, the riotous 'She's On It' (based on an AC/DC sample) was a genuine sensation, leading to

BEASTIE BOYS: First punks, then rappers, now industry moguls

a tour with none other than Madonna. A jaunt with Run DMC helped matters along even further, and all this exposure led to a deal with Columbia, who released the incredible *Licensed To Ill* in 1986.

A global hit, *Licensed To Ill* went platinum in two months and remains the fastest-selling debut album in Columbia's history. A barrage of juvenile knob references, primitive rhymes and semi-hardcore riffing, the record touched a nerve in teenage listeners worldwide, many of whom went on to form bands featured in this book. A touch of controversy was caused by the frat-boy sexism of songs like 'Girls', which helped sales along nicely, as well as the eye-opening cover art, which depicted a crashed plane. The Beasties' penchant for wearing Volkswagen badges on necklaces led to a feeding-frenzy of attacks on Golfs and Polos worldwide, leading many an enraged VW owner to wire his car up to the mains as a deterrent to thieves.

All this teenage hysteria – plus the Beastie Boys' live show, which featured semi-naked girls writhing in cages – meant that the follow-up album, *Paul's Boutique*, was a shock for many fans, with its serious, almost obscure sounds and general air of maturity. The band had enlisted the help of the Dust Brothers production duo, who had laced the album with psychedelic samples, much to the bemusement of the rap fans who had expected more simple riffs and toilet humour. *Paul's Boutique* failed to match its predecessor's success – although the revisionist view now is that it was a seminal album, leading to the success of Beck and other professional obscurists – and many observers consigned the Beastie Boys to career oblivion.

However, the trio displayed some native cunning and immediately started to operate on a wider level. A record label, Grand Royal, was set up; Horovitz acted in films such as *A Kiss Before Dying*; Diamond founded a clothing line, X-Large; and the band built their own studio. Wisely, the next album, 1992's *Check Your Head*, was a return to the Beasties' punk roots, also utilising the talents of keyboard player Money Mark. A deft fusion of rock, punk, funk and hip-hop, the record inspired many a fledgling nu-metal act and remains an understated classic to this day.

Fans gravitated to the band once again, and 1994's *Ill Communication* went double platinum, while the *Some Old Bullshit* hardcore collection, a headlining place on the Lollapalooza festival, the launch of the *Grand Royal* magazine and Adam Yauch's move into Buddhist activity kept the band's profile at maximum.

Recent activities have included a 1999 best-of, *The Sounds of Science*, the founding of the Tibetan Freedom Festival to benefit Yauch's Milarepa Fund, high-profile marriages and a successful studio album, *Hello Nasty*. All this has made the Beastie Boys probably the coolest band in the world, although the band has its critics: the threesome's request to The Prodigy not to play their 'Smack My Bitch Up' single in 1998 on a shared festival bill led to accusations of hypocrisy – the Beasties did have the chicks-in-cages debacle on their CV, after all.

HOW DID THE BEASTIE BOYS INFLUENCE NU-METAL?

Profoundly. No-one mixed rap and rock as cleverly as they did in the Eighties, and in doing so, the Beastie Boys showed many metallers the way forward.

WHY SHOULD WE CARE ABOUT THE BEASTIE BOYS?

Because they mixed and matched musical styles like no band before or since, leading directly to the anything-goes mentality of today's songwriters.

NIRVANA

THE PIONEERS OF RAW, AGONISED EMOTION IN MUSIC

WHO WERE NIRVANA?

A trio from the logging town of Aberdeen, near Seattle, Washington, whose small-town resentment laid the template for dozens of the bands in this book. Nirvana were single-handedly responsible for the rise of the grunge movement and the redefinition of the word 'Seattle' for thousands of music fans. The band's career is essentially the tragic story of singer and guitarist Kurt Cobain, who was unable to endure the devastating conditions that sudden, unprecedented fame placed on his shoulders and who subsequently chose to escape those pressures in the most permanent way of all.

Cobain, the product of a broken home and a childhood spent living with various relatives, met bassist Krist Novoselic in 1985. Both shared a love of American hardcore punk bands such as the Melvins, with whom the duo became firm friends. Cobain had played in various bands, including an act called Fecal Matter, and the pair decided to set up an outfit called The Stiff Woodies, with which Cobain played drums. Various personnel changes took place and in 1987 the band was rechristened Nirvana, with Kurt moving to guitar and vocals.

Local gigs led to a demo with producer Jack Endino, who passed the tape to Jonathan Poneman of the Seattle label Sub

Pop. Poneman offered Nirvana a deal and a single, a version of Shocking Blue's 'Love Buzz', was released in December 1988. A debut album, *Bleach*, was recorded on a shoestring and issued in early 1989, leading to some radio play and tours, which featured second guitarist Jason Everman, later of Soundgarden and then Mindfunk.

Bleach sold respectably and Nirvana enlisted the help of producer Butch Vig (now of Garbage), who recorded another demo, which led to a deal with the DGC label. Drummer Dave Grohl, of the hardcore band Scream, was also recruited at this time. The band recorded an album, *Nevermind*, with Vig and released it in September 1991.

This enormous adulation was impossible for Cobain to handle, and he rapidly developed a crippling heroin addiction, leading to salivating tabloid rumours that the drug was also being used by his pregnant wife, Hole singer Courtney Love. Kurt often complained of stomach pains and began to gain a reputation as a self-destructive, erratic figure constantly on the verge of breakdown.

The fans were kept happy with a 1992 rarities collection, *Incesticide*, and a split single, 'Oh, The Guilt' with The Jesus Lizard, until the release the following year of *In Utero*, a dark, anguished album recorded with Big Black guitarist Steve Albini and remastered by R.E.M. producer

NIRVANA: Reluctant, hair-metal-slaying icons

To the band's shock, the album became not just an unexpected success or even a national sensation, but a genuinely planetary phenomenon, going triple platinum in America alone in a matter of months and even displacing Michael Jackson's *Dangerous* album from the top of the charts. The album's enormous success was driven by its opening song, 'Smells Like Teen Spirit', a song that has become a youth anthem like few others and which influenced much of the rock music made in the early Nineties. MTV adopted the video as its own and all forms of media rushed to worship at the altar of Nirvana.

Scott Litt. A tour saw Cobain veering unsteadily from city to city, overdosing on heroin in May and threatening suicide soon after. However, an MTV *Unplugged* session showed him on healthy, if fragile, form.

Fans were shocked, therefore, by the sequence of events that occurred in spring 1994. Cobain attempted suicide in Rome in February; threatened to kill himself the following month, but was talked out of it by police; entered rehab in late March; escaped the following week; was filed missing by his mother on April 4; and committed suicide at his home the next day. The music world was profoundly rocked by his death and Cobain was posthumously elevated to an almost messianic status by Nirvana's legions of fans.

Novoselic and Grohl elected, wisely, not to continue under the Nirvana name and after the release of *MTV Unplugged In New York* (1994) and a live album, *From The Muddy Banks Of The Wishkah* (1996), activities ceased. Grohl went on to front the very successful Foo Fighters.

HOW DID NIRVANA INFLUENCE NU-METAL?

In many ways: lyrically, musically and socially – the last because they set up the conditions for nu-metal to be formed. People have always wanted to lose themselves in dark music: that's a well-known fact, and it's nothing new. Nirvana just brought the opportunity to do so a lot closer for most people.

JANE'S ADDICTION

THE BAND THAT BROUGHT WEIRDNESS TO METAL

WHO WERE THEY?

Formed in 1984 in Los Angeles, and consisting of ex-Psi Com singer Perry Farrell, guitarist Dave Navarro, bassist Eric Avery and drummer Stephen Perkins, Jane's Addiction were a weird band who (like fellow Californians Faith No More) initially scared a lot of people off with their intense brew of metal, punk, jazz and even folk influences.

However, those that *did* get the Jane's Addiction bug were fiercely vocal in support of their chosen band, who had released a live album recorded at the Roxy in Hollywood, and a buzz developed

JANE'S ADDICTION: The weirdest rock band ever?

WHY SHOULD WE CARE ABOUT NIRVANA?

The story of Nirvana is pretty much the story of grunge, which they brought to the mainstream and which died along with Cobain. Grunge killed old metal, forcing nu-metal to be born. If you're a nu-metal fan, you should care a *lot* about Nirvana, even if the band's music isn't to your taste, because nu-metal owes grunge its very existence.

rapidly on the LA club scene, leading to a bidding war. This was eventually won by Warners, who released *Nothing's Shocking* in 1988. Slightly controversial in content and cover art, the album spent over six months in the charts and led to the formation of an international fanbase.

Ritual De Lo Habitual was an even more successful record, released two years later, but Farrell felt that the band had run its course and set up a festival, Lollapalooza, to host the band's farewell tour. After the band split in 1991, the Lollapalooza concept refused to die, however, and went on to become an annual fixture for the next few years, showcasing all kinds of new bands and ultimately being supplanted by the various Ozzfests, Tattoo The Earths, Family Values and Warped tours that sprang up in its wake.

Farrell went on to form Porno For Pyros and Navarro spent a couple of years in the Red Hot Chili Peppers. It was assumed that Jane's Addiction was permanently out of action until 2001, when rumours spread that Farrell was planning to reform this legendary band.

HOW DID JANE'S ADDICTION INFLUENCE NU-METAL?

By making it the norm to mix a variety of styles into the heavy metal idiom, and look stylish at the same time. Without Jane's Addiction there would be no art-metal of any kind (Tool, Orgy, Marilyn Manson).

WHY SHOULD WE CARE ABOUT JANE'S ADDICTION?

Because they had courage, like all true pioneers.

ROSS ROBINSON

THE MOST INFLUENTIAL PRODUCER IN METAL TODAY

WHO IS HE?

The American producer Ross Robinson is a well-known figure in modern metal. Having produced several key albums by influential artists, he's stamped his instantly-recognisable mark on popular music in the same way that Phil Spector did in the Sixties, John Leckie did in the Seventies and Trevor Horn did in the Eighties. But more than this, he is also responsible for the discovery and elevation to the public eye of various key players, scouting for talent and signing them to his own label, I Am, which was once partnered with Roadrunner and which currently enjoys a mutually profitable relationship with Virgin.

Robinson grew up in the desert towns of California and played guitar in the obscure speed metal band Détente, which released an album, *Recognize No Authority*, in 1986, the last great year of thrash metal. He also formed a progressive thrash band, Catalepsy (which later changed its name to

Murdercar) with future Machine Head drummer Dave McClain. Neither outfit was particularly successful, however, and he moved into producing.

Early projects included the WASP album *The Crimson Idol* in 1992, which he worked on as a studio intern, and a demo with the then-unsigned Fear Factory. Robinson's big break came, however, when he witnessed a band called LAPD (it meant Love And Peace, Dude – I know, I know) playing live at a local club in Los Angeles. Impressed by the guitarists' downtuned sound, he invited the band to work on a demo with him: the results were impressive. Robinson also managed to persuade them to change their name: the new moniker they chose was Korn. Their self-titled debut, which Ross produced, was infused with hip-hop and was almost solely responsible for the tidal wave of change that subsequently swept the metal scene.

Korn made Robinson's name and he went on to produce seminal records such as Limp Bizkit's debut album, *Three Dollar Bill, Y'All$*, and both of Slipknot's major-label records, as well as working with Sepultura, Soulfly, Tura Satana and dozens of smaller outfits such as the brand-new British band Vex Red. A key development was his discovery of Amen, whose two albums to date, *Amen* (1999) and *We Have Come For*

ROSS ROBINSON: It's all his fault

Your Parents (2000) have been recognised as pioneering in the field of punk-metal. Robinson himself labelled the latter record as the most intense album that has ever been released by a major label, a claim which holds a lot of truth to this day.

The secret of Robinson's success as a producer is twofold. Firstly, and most obviously, is the sound he achieves: most prominent are the visceral guitar riffs and the crystal-clear percussion. Secondly, Ross draws out the inner rage from the performers, pushing them to limits they had previously thought impossible, enraging or provoking them to find out what gives them their strength – but always with a sense of support. He famously threw a pot plant at Slipknot drummer Joey Jordison to keep him focused, and has left the console to join the players slamming in the studio in mid-take. All of this is designed to take the performers away from the sterile studio environment, to a place where they can play at their hardest and most powerful. It's a long way from the traditional producer's role, stuck in the console room behind a sheet of glass.

In the last year or so, however, Robinson has evidenced some dissatisfaction with the sound he has created. The idea of nu-metal (often dubbed 'sports metal' or 'Adidas metal' by sarcastic onlookers unimpressed by Korn's choice of leisurewear) being his responsibility is clearly one that irks him, and the fact that there are now so many bands emulating the style he pioneered is also a factor. His influences come from the old school – speed metal such as Slayer (with whom he discussed a possible production role in 2000), and grindcore bands such as Carcass, whose work he holds in high esteem. He was even said to be considering a production role with the Norwegian progressive black metallers Emperor, although penetrating that notoriously closed scene will be a tricky task.

However, he remains much in demand as a producer. This current dissatisfaction may merely be a symptom of his hunger for progression – which is what made him such a talented producer in the first place.

HOW DID HE INFLUENCE NU-METAL?

The whole sound of nu-metal is Robinson's work. Without him, the entire canon of modern metal would sound radically different, and several of the most important bands would not exist.

WHY SHOULD WE CARE ABOUT ROSS ROBINSON?

Because he cares about what he does enough to let it go. Respect is due.

ROADRUNNER

THE LABEL THAT BROUGHT NU-METAL TO YOUR STEREO

WHAT IS ROADRUNNER?

Although the nu-metal movement consists of hundreds of bands signed to dozens of different record labels, the regularity with which the name of Roadrunner Records appears makes it more or less the most important company on this particular scene. It's still a company, of course, with corporate objectives, which means that the bottom line is still the most important factor – but it has shaped the music like no other. Small enough to handle its artist roster with some human warmth but large enough to stay afloat in this most perilous of industries, the label has consistently been at the forefront of metal.

Roadrunner started life in 1981, founded in Amsterdam by its chairman, Cees Wessels. At that time it was known for licensing American extreme metal for Europe: records by Metallica, Slayer and Megadeth appeared through Roadrunner after it formed business links with US labels such as Relativity, Triple X and SST.

As metal itself developed, so did Roadrunner. With the rise of death metal in the early Nineties, the label – which had opened a New York office in late 1986 – signed influential acts such as Deicide, Malevolent Creation and the newly-formed Fear Factory. Sepultura also joined the roster, with over four million records sold through the company.

But it was the latter half of the decade that saw the company step up to the frontline. Goth-metallers Coal Chamber and Type O Negative had seen some significant success, as did Machine Head, but Slipknot's debut album propelled Roadrunner into an entirely different league, helped along by the enormous interest in Amen and Soulfly. Many of

OZZFEST: Bringing nu-metal to your door

the new breed had been signed through the company's new Los Angeles office, opened in 1996. International offices had also been established.

All this success led cynics to refer to 'Roadrunner bands' as a group of acts whose music – the 'Roadrunner sound', often the work of Ross Robinson and other big producers such as Colin Richardson – you could safely predict. But this was just the result of the rise of nu-metal, and the label's eye for talent. Roadrunner remains the key label for this type of music, although as half its stock was sold to Island in 2001 it's impossible to say how long its approach can remain truly independent.

HOW DID THE COMPANY INFLUENCE NU-METAL?

It made nu-metal what it is by identifying the key bands and bringing them to the public eye, with only faith to go on. Big labels don't do that. Small labels *can't* do that.

WHY SHOULD WE CARE ABOUT ROADRUNNER?

Because what it does, and the way it does it, makes the world of metal that bit more exciting.

OZZFEST

A TRAVELLING CIRCUS OF MADNESS, BRINGING METAL TO THE MASSES

WHAT IS THE OZZFEST?

An annual festival organised by veteran metal guru Ozzy Osbourne, his wife and manager Sharon and Ozzy's band Black Sabbath. The show usually features up to 20 bands and plays in various countries: since the first tour in 1997, it's become a genuine institution, helped along by the demise of the once-legendary Castle Donington show and the de-metalisation of the once very heavy Reading Festival. It has also spawned a few live albums and the usual range of merchandise.

The bands that play are largely nu-metal and hardcore outfits, with a few old-school thrash bands thrown into the mix for good measure. Notable appearances have been made by Marilyn Manson, Sepultura, Neurosis, Coal Chamber, Biohazard, Slayer, Powerman 5000, Earth Crisis, Fear Factory, Soulfly, Disturbed, Papa Roach, Slipknot, Tool and dozens of others both in and out of this book. The new bands are said to be chosen by Osbourne's teenage son, Jack, a nu-metal kid of some perception, and the show remains the thinking metaller's ideal day out.

HOW DOES IT INFLUENCE NU-METAL?

The bands that play on the Ozzfest get more exposure than they would anywhere else. The fans buy their records. The bands become successful. The scene itself is changed as a result. See? Make no mistake, the Ozzfest may be just a concert – but its power is real.

WHY SHOULD WE CARE ABOUT THE OZZFEST?

Because there's a real sense of old and new working together, unselfishly. Who says the music industry is always cynical?

A-Z OF NU-METAL BANDS

A

www.a-communication.com

Sometimes referred to as the British equivalent of the no-brainer frat-punk outfit Blink 182, the guaranteed-first-in-any-phone-book A fuse a whole host of influences into their sound – Beastie Boys, Beck, Jane's Addiction, Blur – and were welcomed with open arms in the mid-Nineties by rock festival crowds. Consisting of the three Suffolk-based Perry brothers, Jason (vocals), Adam (drums) and Giles (keyboards), plus guitarist Mark Chapman and bassist Daniel P. Carter, the band signed to London in 1996 and issued a debut album, *How Ace Are Buildings*, recorded in California with Offspring producer Thom Wilson. Tours with the briefly reformed Sex Pistols and teenage never-weres Symposium followed – the fans were clearly delighted with the often silly, always entertaining quirkiness of the A recipe and the band's profile grew rapidly.

The second album, *Monkey Kong* (named in tribute to the immortal Eighties Nintendo game *Donkey Kong*) contained the insane eccentricities of its predecessor, but the new songwriting had a noticeable touch of sophistication, with electronic and turntable sounds more in evidence. Tours with Feeder, Reef and Ash ensued and performances at major British festivals kept the flag flying, while a suitably bizarre remix album ensured that the band never became predictable. Deeply odd.

A PERFECT CIRCLE

www.aperfectcircle.com

Among the more cerebral, experimental bands found in the broad church of nu-metal is A Perfect Circle, which started as a side project for Tool singer Maynard James Keenan and has developed into an art-rock project in its own right. The often melancholy, gothic-sounding songs are written by sometime Tool/Fishbone guitar tech Billy Howerdel, while the other members of the Circle are Paz Lenchantin (bass/violin), Troy van Leeuwen (ex-Failure and Vandals, guitar) and Josh Freese (ex-Guns N'Roses, drums).

The band first formed in 1997 after Keenan, exhausted after a protracted legal wrangle between Tool and an industry organisation, took some time off to recuperate. Howerdel approached him with some songs and the singer, eager to focus on non-Tool-related activities, assembled a band. Rumours of APC activity intrigued Tool fans, but no live dates took place until August 1999, when Keenan unveiled his new act at LA's Viper Club. Reception was positive among fans and critics and an

A: The strange face of British nu-metal

album, the very dark *Mer De Noms*, was recorded and released nine months later: Howerdel's experience as a co-writer for Smashing Pumpkins and Nine Inch Nails was apparent in the brooding, introspective set of songs (no sports-metal chart hits here) and angst-ridden teenagers worldwide embraced it with relish.

Tool subsequently regrouped after their five-year rest and it is currently not known if A Perfect Circle will work together in the future or remain a one-off project. But if it's a fix of doom-laden bedsit metal you're after, *Mer De Noms* will be just the ticket.

ALIEN ANT FARM

www.alienantfarm.com

Quirky without being annoying, Alien Ant Farm are among the most inventive of the nu-metal crowd, experimenting with funk, unusual percussion parts and straight-ahead riffing to produce the nu-metal equivalent of say, the Red Hot Chili Peppers. Formed in Riverside, California in 1996, the band's first influences were singer Dryden Mitchell's father's records, by acts as disparate as The Beatles, Frank Zappa, Tracy Chapman and Edie Brickell. Guitarist Terry Corso was more of an orthodox headbanger: his mother used to provide him with Kiss records – little knowing, perhaps, what lay ahead.

Chick label in 1999. A heavy, melodic album, it won the title of Best Independent Album at the LA Music Awards.

Embarking on prolonged touring in 2000, AAF built a reputation for their live shows. In true nu-metal style, a darker side was emerging: Mitchell was writing new material from the throes of a broken relationship, which revealed itself in his openly angst-ridden lyrics. The big break came when Papa Roach – who had become firm friends with the Farm while slogging it out on the Californian club circuit in the late Nineties – signed them to their Dreamworks-partnered label, New Noize. The two bands had supported each other when touring each other's hometowns, and a pact had long been struck between both outfits that whoever broke first would help the other one out.

ALIEN ANT FARM: Hey Annie, are you OK? Apparently so...

Teaming up with bassist Tye Zamora and drummer Mike Cosgrove and settling on a name (Corso: "Wouldn't it be cool if the human species were placed on earth and cultivated by alien intelligence? Maybe the aliens added us to an atmosphere that was suitable for us, and they've been watching us develop and colonize, kind of like what a kid does with an ant farm, where the aliens are the kids and humans are the ants" – in case you were wondering) the band released their debut album, the superbly-titled *Greatest Hits*, on their own

The AAF major-label debut was released in March 2001 and was titled *ANThology*: produced by Jay Baumgardner (Papa Roach, Orgy, Coal Chamber), it was a slicker, more inventive record than their first album and was snapped up by the Californian fanbase, with plenty of interest on the European festival scene developing by the summer. A major tour with the Roach was scheduled at the time of writing. Alien Ant Farm, it seems, have the gravitas to succeed longer than most, despite their occasionally juvenile wit:

ANThology shows they have a deeper side than the usual frat-boy arsing about that all nu-metal bands seem to go through. And in summer 2001, their beefed-up cover of Michael Jackson's 'Smooth Criminal' landed them in the charts: a development that not even the most perspicacious industry observer could have predicted.

AMEN

www.whoresofhollywood.com

Perhaps the angriest band in this book apart from Slipknot, with whom they share certain ideological and political opinions, Amen are the reincarnation of punk in nu-metal form. Punk, that is, in the most advised sense of the word: after all, there's no Sex Pistols-like musical incompetence here, no Conflict-style provincial anarchy and certainly no Offspring-type radio-friendliness. No – Amen are punk because they resent everything. No less a punk icon than Pistols guitarist Steve Jones pointed out in 2000 that "Amen's more pissed off than we ever were". This rage will take them a long way, it appears: after two albums (and one

scheduled for release in early 2002), the band are flying high as darlings of the metal press: their stature is helped along nicely by the charisma of their frontman Casey Chaos, a troubled, outspoken figure whose pale, moon-like face is often to be seen staring from magazine covers.

Amen took its first steps in the mid-Nineties when Chaos met guitarist Paul Fig and began to write some fairly raw tunes. Ex-Snot performers Sonny Mayo, bassist John Tumor and drummer Larkin were recruited and a fuller sound began to take shape. More akin to late-Seventies punk aggression than conventional metal ("We're not a metal band," insisted Casey in the summer of 2001 – he has a point, although it's a debatable one), Amen soon attracted the attention of über-producer Ross Robinson, and became the first band to sign to his imprint, I Am Records, which at the time had a business partnership with Roadrunner.

Amen's self-titled debut album was released in early 1999 and was a landmark recording, with Robinson visibly awed by the band's phenomenal energy and commitment. Chaos gave his all in the vocal booth (stories, possibly apocryphal,

emerged concerning his near-hospitalisation during the recording, such was his anguish) and on subsequent tours: crowds were shocked when he cut himself with broken glass during certain shows in an attempt to externalise his inner pain.

The causes of all this agony have never been fully explained, but Chaos indicates his despair at the world in his lyrics, which were clearer still on the next Amen record, *We Have Come For Your Parents* (recorded once again by Robinson, but released through Virgin, to whom I Am had switched allegiance). "This is the most violent record ever to be released by a major label. There is no record on the planet ever made that hits the same level of intensity," reported Robinson of the album. Said Chaos: "The American dream has instilled in our culture a raw thirst for fame and money, as defined by Britney Spears and the Calvin Kleins of the world, whom I consider to be the real murderers at

ANTIPRODUCT: Beware their vomit

large... We are told to pray to false icons, we are told to eat, breathe, walk, look a certain way – and it's all lies. It's not who we really are. It's not who I am. That's what punk rock is all about – a musical form to express outrage at the bourgeois pigs' attempt to define society by hiding the truth."

Songs such as 'Piss Virus', a rant against America's dehumanised computer culture and 'CK Killer', a rant against America's, er, dehumanised fashion culture, showed the world's metallers quite clearly where Amen's vitriol was aimed, and the record sold in droves. Clearly there is still room

for anger in metal, and what's more, it is obviously a commercial bonus. The question of how long such fury can be sustained is a moot one, of course: but when revered old-school punkers such as the Damned's drummer Rat Scabies come out with statements such as "Amen is the punkest, heaviest thing out of America since the Stooges and the MC5", it's not an issue that is ever dwelled upon for long.

ANTIPRODUCT

www.antiproduct.com

Situated somewhere between serious nu-metal band with a political message and studenty high-jinks cabaret act, Antiproduct is the British project of ex-Life, Sex and Death singer and guitarist Alex Kane, who goes by the name A. Product and who was also known a few years ago for his Clam Abuse band with ex-Wildhearts singer Ginger. The other Antiproduct members are Clare (guitar), Milena Yum (keyboards), Toshi (bass) and Simon (drums).

The band first began touring in the summer of 2000, having released an album, *Consume And Die... The Rest is All Fun*, through Cargo. Kane immediately attracted some attention on the release of the double A-side single 'Hey Let's Get It On'/'Best Day Of Your Life' by standing naked on top of a van and shouting at passers-by through a megaphone as it drove through London – although it's doubtful that any of the cops who cautioned him afterwards were converted to the AP cause. He also managed, it's said, to vomit on the well-known media figure Chris Evans from the top of the same van, as well as on a group of fans waiting for a Slipknot concert – ironically, the masked Iowans are renowned for their onstage barrage of body fluids. Kane's appearance could have been construed as a taster, perhaps?

After the moderate success of the *This Is How We Buy The Van* EP in 2001, surprise endorsements came from the Bass brewing company, which created a special Antiproduct Ale in their honour, and the adult magazine *Mayfair*, which ran features on the band in two consecutive issues. Antiproduct has also compiled a video, *A Day At The Office*, which remains strangely compelling viewing for metal fans who find Gwar just too sedate.

APARTMENT 26

www.apartment26.com

Like their countrymen Pitchshifter, the highly eclectic Apartment 26 infuse a wide range of styles into their aggressive, unpredictable sound, including drum'n'bass and techno elements. Basically a metal band, however, the band – Biff (vocals), Jon Greasley (guitar), Louis Cruden (bass), AC Huckvale (keyboards) and Kevin Temple (drums) – recorded and self-released an EP in 1999, which sold in significant quantities when they landed a spot on the second stage at the Ozzfest of that year.

Solid touring with heavyweights such as Powerman 5000, Fu Manchu, Sevendust, Henry Rollins and System Of A Down put them in a position of some authority, consolidated by the appearance of their songs on the soundtracks to the films *Heavy Metal 2* and *Mission Impossible: 2*. A full album, *Hallucinating*, was released in 2000 and has kept the band on a constant upward path, with a spot on the Ozzfest in 2001 yet another indicator that they may be a band to be reckoned with for some time.

AREA 54: Simultaneously extreme and 'nu'

AREA 54

www.area54.co.uk

Formed around the talents of Essex-born guitarist and vocalist Lakis Kyriacou, Area 54 state that their aim is to revive melodic metal and that their influences include rock (Guns N'Roses), death metal (At The Gates, Death), black metal (Cradle Of Filth) and old-school thrash (Metallica, Megadeth). They also include classical, funk, drum'n'bass and psychedelic elements in

their sound – this diversity of influence is the key that lets them through the nu-metal door.

After several line-up changes, the band ultimately became Kyriacou plus drummer Rob Hillman (sometime of the very black metal-sounding Cruciferous), bassist Laura Salmon and guitarist Steve Martin (who replaced Adrian Longley shortly after the band's inception). The band started gigging in 1997 and recorded a demo, *Fear Inside*, which led to a deal with Dream Catcher and a debut album, *No Visible Scars*, in April 2000. The deal came about after *Metal Hammer/Total Rock* journalist Malcolm Dome passed a copy of the demo onto the label.

A second album is underway and Area 54's future looks promising, with festival appearances also confirmed for 2001 and a label to throw at journalists: they claim to be part of the "Nu-Wave Of British Heavy Metal". Now *that's* initiative for you.

AT THE DRIVE-IN

www.atthedrive-in.net

At one time tipped by those in the know to be the next band up for the nu-metal crown, At The Drive-In (named after a Poison lyric, tellingly enough) were a five-piece from the dusty environs of El Paso, Texas, who reaped the rewards of being signed to what was perhaps the world's coolest record label - Grand Royal, owned by the Beastie Boys, which folded in September 2001. But it was a long ride: the band first formed in 1993 around the nucleus of guitarist Jim Ward. A 7", amusingly titled 'Hell Paso', was self-released in November 1994, followed by another, 'Alfaro Vive, Carajo', the following summer, after which the band famously toured the USA in a a battered Ford van.

The indie labels Flipside and Offtime were attracted by the rapidly-growing ATDI profile, and each issued an EP (*Acrobatic Tenement* and *El Gran Orgo* respectively) in 1997. The year also saw the band tour extensively and the formation of Ward's own label, Headquarter Records. A third label, Fearless, offered to fund an album after seeing ATDI perform in support to the still-obscure Supernova: *In/Casino/Out* was recorded in June 1998 and showcased a band hardened by constant touring: the producer was Alex Newport

(Fudge Tunnel/Nailbomb) and the record was their biggest success to date, garnering positive reviews nationwide and securing slots on the Californian This Ain't No Picnic festival with Sonic Youth.

Fearless stepped in once again for an EP, *Vaya*, released in July 1999, after which At The Drive-In moved to Den Records, which contacted producer Ross Robinson and set up a session. A recording duly took place in New York: all parties were delighted with the result and the band decided that Ross would be the man to produce their major-label debut. On the point of entering Robinson's preferred studio, Indigo Ranch in Malibu, ATDI received a call from none other than Rage

Beastie Boys. Stranger things have happened in the world of metal, but not many.

The band has gone from strength to strength, but it was a long time coming – and their status near the top of the nu-metal tree was not made any easier by the cat-calls of one or two long-time fans who have labelled them sell-outs for signing to a label with major distribution. Unfortunately, in the wake of Grand Royal's collapse came news that ATDI had decided to take an indefinite break from the record/tour/record cycle, citing exhaustion as the reason. Many observers regard this as equivalent to a permanent split, but don't be too sure - this is one band that fans cannot afford to write off.

AT THE DRIVE IN: Nu-metal almost-rans

Against The Machine, who requested the band's support presence on an imminent mini-tour. This is not the kind of call that an aspiring metal band declines, and so Ross agreed to delay the sessions until January 2000.

The seven-week recording yielded some spectacular results: the album, *Relationship Of Command*, was an uncompromising beast laced with Robinson's organic production touches and mixed down by Andy Wallace, who – like Robinson – could boast production duties for Sepultura on his CV. As the record neared completion, word came that the Den label was about to merge with Grand Royal – which is how the band found itself signed up with the

ATARI TEENAGE RIOT

www.atariteenageriot.de

A German band that balances enormous guitar riffs and metallic trademarks such as screamed or shouted vocals with pure electronica, Atari Teenage Riot is usually referred to as a techno outfit despite the metal elements of its music. Because of this deft combination of riffing and sequenced beats, fans of extreme metal and extreme electronica cite ATR as a seminal act – not for nothing is 'hardcore' an adjective applied to both techno and rock.

However, the categorisation of the band is a mere side issue in contrast with ATR's primary function, which is as an aggressively anarchist collective with the destruction of conventional social and political structures its declared aim. 'Riot sounds lead to riots!' is the slogan of the main composer and performer Alec Empire, whose perseverance (he has released over 20 independent EPs and several albums under his own name for the Chrome, Mille Plateaux and Riot Beats labels, as well as under the aegis of Atari Teenage Riot) and penchant for uncompromising public statements has made him something of a cult figure.

Founded in 1992 after Empire and fellow noise-mongers Carl Crack and Hanin Elias had been releasing underground techno for some years, the aim behind Atari Teenage Riot was to make tangible the excitement they had experienced on hearing punk and hip-hop for the first time. Although other pioneers of electronica such as Moby were doing much the same thing, ATR deliberately chose to make their music as gut-wrenchingly abrasive as possible, with layers of grindcore guitars, distorted percussion and throat-shredding screams.

Their political stance was immediately made clear on a debut single, 'Hunt The Nazis', released as a protest against the neo-Nazi movement, which Empire claims has quadrupled in size since the reunification of Germany. Other releases followed on the Force, Inc. label before a surprise move to the major Phonogram company. Two EPs, *Not Your Business* and the slightly naively-titled *Kids R United* were subsequently issued, followed by an extended tour to ecstatic (if shell-shocked) club crowds.

However, Empire took his band back from Phonogram, claiming that the label had tried to impose commercial restraints on his songwriting. But Phonogram had advanced a significant sum of money, supposedly to be used on the recording of a full-length album, which Alec chose to spend (allegedly, m'lud) on the launch of a label, Digital Hardcore. The live schedule was ratcheted up to a Transit-shagging 300 shows per year and ATR went on to support a variety of bands, including Dinosaur Jr.

1994 saw the Ataris move away from the techno genre (a single, 'Raverbashing', was their final raised finger to the scene which had spawned them) and the following year, an album was finally recorded. *Delete Yourself* was a typically exhausting listen, but succeeded in attracting the attention of none other than the Beastie Boys, who signed ATR to their newly-formed Grand Royal label (later to become the home of At The Drive-In, see above).

By this point the band seemed to have become a permanent fixture, issuing singles in an apparently unceasing sequence. Highlights of the next couple of years included a co-composition with Slayer, 'No Remorse (I Wanna Die)', for the *Spawn* soundtrack, plus a tour with Rage Against The Machine and a US tour with labelmates Ec8or and Shizuo. A fourth musician, Nic Endo, was also recruited in time for more albums (*60 Second Wipe Out* and *Live in Philadelphia 1997*) and a tour with the appropriately electro-metal Nine Inch Nails.

ATARI TEENAGE RIOT: Do not mess with this band

Recent activities have included the release of the *Rage* EP, which featured the talents of Rage Against The Machine guitarist Tom Morello. The ATR urge to destroy appears to be as powerful as ever, judging by Empire's words on his website, which include the statements "Boredom has led to fascism not hate. Nationalism must die! Capitalism must die! This system must be destroyed", "Damaging public institutions and places costs the state money that helps the system to implode!" and, most intimidatingly, the evidently enraged

"Do not vote! Let's start riots ! Set police cars on fire! Celebrate girls! Respect terrorists! Smash TV sets! Destroy all prisons! Destroy Christian morals!".

Sadly, Carl Crack committed suicide in September 2001, although it is unlikely that a band of this degree of energy will be sidelined for long.

AUTONOMY

www.autonomy1.com

Nu-metal is predominantly an American phenomenon (the British equivalent is more punk-orientated), so it's always a pleasure when a credible UK outfit comes to prominence, as has been the case with Autonomy, formed in 1998 in Daventry, Northamptonshire, by two singers, Terry Muller and Jay Spencer. The county had already produced two hard-hitting acts in the form of Raging Speedhorn and Defenestration (all three bands label themselves 'extreme nu-metal'), but Autonomy's initial approach was less aggressive, focusing more on the hip-hop beats of Limp Bizkit and their baseball-capped brethren. However, as the band gained experience, their sound drew on tougher influences and the music subsequently became much more uncompromising. Guitarist Matt Cosentino added a much harder edge to the sound, and the recruitment of Paul (bass) and Rich (drums) led to the current line-up.

Autonomy's big break came when a three-track demo, recorded in 1999, led to an appearance on the Unsigned Band Stage at the Manchester 'In The City' gig in September 2000: a label race of sorts ensued, with Nottingham's Earache signing the band up over bigger players such as Columbia. The following January Terry was replaced by Olly Eldershaw and the band began preparing for the recording of a self-titled debut album. Eldershaw himself was replaced by LA emigrant 'Soup' Carpenter during pre-production – the newbie's prime claim to fame was that he once shared a room with Deftones frontman Chino Moreno. Console duties were scheduled for David Dominguez, sometime studio engineer with Papa Roach and Limp Bizkit. Time will tell if Autonomy can live up to their early promise.

BIG DUMB FACE: Wes Borland, now free of Limp Bizkit, but still looking pretty bizarre

BIG DUMB FACE

www.bigdumbface.com

The side-project of the eccentric ex-Limp Bizkit guitarist Wes Borland, Big Dumb Face is a bizarre, semi-serious group of musicians consisting of Borland himself (under the stage name Tongue Of Colicab – he also used this name on sleevenotes with his old band), his brother Scott (The Cardboard Urinal, guitar) and their high-school friends Kyle Weeks

arose in 2000 between Bizkit tours, and sessions took place in Borland's home studio, with the guitarist arranging, recording and mixing the material himself. The result, *Duke Lion Fights The Terror*, was released by Geffen in March 2001, to mixed reviews: a frenzied, multifaceted record, it veers between Scandinavian black metal ('Burgaveist') and Mr. Bungle-style weirdcore ('Robot').

No-one seems to know entirely what to make of the album, although the unexpected support of various members of Slipknot (who have generally not been on good terms with Limp Bizkit over the years) may be some consolation for Borland, who, in any case, no longer has his planet-straddling main band to worry about.

BIOHAZARD: The original kings of NY hardcore

(The Three Headed Demetrian Pup, guitar) and Greg Isabel (Joe Couch, drums). Chris Gibbs (Moivet O'Sphelvey) plays bass. Like the Bizkit, BDF is based in Jacksonville, Florida: Chris, Scott and Greg also play in a local band, the Chad Jasmine Factor.

The origins of Big Dumb Face lie in a school band, Goatslayer, which disbanded when Borland toured with Limp Bizkit. As the chart-metallers' profile grew, Wes never fully abandoned the idea of a Goatslayer project and spent his off-time on the road writing songs and designing album artwork. A window of opportunity finally

BIOHAZARD

www.biohazard.com

Driven by their immediate environment like no other band in these pages apart from Slipknot, the Brooklyn, New York quartet Biohazard were formed in 1988 by Evan Seinfeld (bass/vocals), Billy Graziadei (guitar/vocals), Bobby Hambel (guitar) and Danny Schuler (drums). Although the band specialise in a hardcore punk/thrash metal approach (the twist being that both Seinfeld and Graziadei handle lead vocals), they also include the occasional rap, which has led many fans to claim that they are the true inventors of rap-metal, and therefore of nu-metal. They're certainly among the handful of acts that can claim such a thing, but it's impossible to be sure.

The Biohazard beginnings were as punk as you like, touring with the crossover kings Cro-Mags and the cartoon thrashers Carnivore (based around the huge Peter Steele, soon to divert his talents into the goth-metallers Type O Negative) and appearing at the Big Apple's famous L'Amour club. The band released an independent album, *Biohazard*, which included the controversial 'Howard Beach', a song addressing a racially-motivated murder in Brooklyn. Although Biohazard have no right-wing opinions, the fact that the object of the song's venom was a black man led to a fascist label being applied to the band.

This undeserved tag lingered until the release of the second Biohazard album, *Urban Discipline*, recorded in two weeks for Roadrunner, with whom the band had signed a one-album deal in 1992. The anti-racism anthem 'Black And White And Red All Over' was Biohazard's direct response to their critics and was a powerful, intelligent song, but the album's high point was 'Punishment', which was accompanied by a memorable video in which Seinfeld et al took to the streets of Kings County.

Both speed metal fans and punks got the Biohazard bug (they toured with Kreator in Europe and Sick Of It All in the States), and even rappers were introduced to the band courtesy of a collaboration with the hip-hop outfit Onyx for the *Judgement Night* soundtrack. All this high-level activity meant that a departure to a major label was appropriate and so the band moved to Warners, recording *State Of The World Address* with Living Colour producer Ed Stasium. The album was toured with Pantera and Sepultura throughout the US and received top-notch reviews, despite some bad press in 1995 when Biohazard's second appearance at the Donington rock festival was cut short by the stage management, panicked by the band's infamous tendency to invite hundreds of fans onstage. Later that year Hambel left the band (the usual 'musical differences' were blamed, with Seinfeld later observing that guitarist and band were "on different paths") and was replaced by ex-Helmet six-stringer Rob Echeverria. Roadrunner issued a live album, *No Holds Barred*, as the new line-up prepared to record their fourth studio album, *New World Disorder*, another long-player received with great acclaim.

More touring followed, this time with Insane Clown Posse and Coal Chamber, in between Seinfeld's recurring cameo as a prison inmate alongside LL Cool J and Treach in the TV drama, *Oz*.

After a period away from the public eye, Biohazard regrouped in 2001 for a new album, *Uncivilization*. Journalists often addressed the newfound prevalence of nu-metal and the band's alleged role as its creators, which Evan once countered with the words, "Biohazard's music isn't any 'type' of music but Biohazard music. I hate the idea of music being labelled 'hip hop', 'metal', 'rap', 'hardcore'. Who cares? I wish people could just see past their preconceptions and see music for what it really is." Fair enough, we say.

BLOODHOUND GANG

www.bloodhoundgang.com

Keeping the frat-boy spirit of the early Beastie Boys alive and spicing it up with a dose of good old-fashioned sex'n'drugs'n'cussin', the Bloodhound Gang are perhaps the most deliberately politically incorrect band in these pages, and the kids love them for it.

The band first convened in 1993, when singer Jimmy Pop Ali and guitarist Lupus (from Philadelphia and LA) recorded two amateur tapes, *Just Another Demo* and *The Original Motion Picture Soundtrack To Hitler's Handicapped Helpers*.

This was followed by an EP, *Dingleberry Haze*: something must have sounded right, because the duo were then signed to Columbia, who released a full-length album, *Use Your Fingers*, which flopped. The Gang were dropped unceremoniously but regrouped with the addition of the fire-breathing bassist (and student friend of Jimmy) Evil Jared Hasselhoff, the drummer Spanky G and a DJ, Q-Ball. Gigs soon took place at New York's renowned CBGBs, to the bemusement of the local patrons.

Recording a second album, the knowingly-titled *One Fierce Beer Coaster*, for the independent Republic label, the Bloodhound Gang were surprised when MTV and radio picked the song 'Fire Water Burn' up and ran with it. Other successful singles included 'Why's Everybody Always Pickin' On Me?' and (cough) 'I Wish I Was Queer So I Could Get Chicks'.

This led to a contract with a larger company, DGC, although the hur-hur

BLOODHOUND GANG: Pure juvenalia

humour remained in full effect for 2000's *Hooray For Boobies* album, which featured a song called 'The Ballad Of Chasey Lain', a homage to the porn actress of the same name.

BOILER ROOM

www.boilerroommusic.com

One of a handful of New York bands that combine hardcore punk with effectively heavy metal riffing, Boiler Room have yet to make it to the big time, although it seems that they have the commitment to do it. Chris Lino (vocals), Rob Caggiano (guitar), James Meselsohn (bass) and Mike Meselsohn (drums) formed in 1996 and started to make demos heavily influenced by the city they lived in, especially in terms of the harsh aural assault of the music.

These recordings attracted the attention of the Tommy Boy label, which offered them a contract: a debut album, *Can't Breathe*, gathered together a set of the demos, polished into shape by Kid Rock producer John Travis and mixed by Phil Nicolo (Life Of Agony, Cypress Hill). Gigs with established venue-fillers such as Static X, Clutch, Type O Negative and King's X – as well as a well-publicised radio showcase with those children of the Korn, Orgy – saw the BR profile rise, and a fanbase has gathered. Maybe it's something in the water over there, but these NY bands seem to be tougher than most – and Boiler Room look set to continue this trend.

BREACH OF TRUST

www.breachoftrust.com

Despite only having recently risen from the murky underground metal scene, the Canadian band Breach Of Trust was in fact formed back in 1994 in the northern environs of La Ronge in Saskatchewan. An indie EP, *Dead Issue*, was releaed the following year, with a single, 'Family', gaining some local airplay.

Tours followed and significant numbers of the EP were sold to warrant a serious effort to break the band, and investors were recruited to fund the recording of a full-length album, *Songs For Dying Nations*, and a North American tour. This took place in 2000 and was, by all accounts, a success.

CAFFEINE

www.evolutional.co.uk/caffeine

Rather winsomely naming themselves after cities for a short period, Caffeine's initial line-up consisted of guitarist J, bassist/vocalist Alain Lovine and drummer Tony Marshall (or – honestly – Sheffield, Rome and London). The trio, based in King's Cross, London, met at an audition for a different band in 1996 and discovered a common passion for Californian punk. Contacting sometime Lemonheads and Symposium producer Julian Standen, the band recorded and released a single, 'Romance', on their own Fluffy Freako label. The song was an instant club hit and attracted offers from several major labels, but the band elected to stick with both Standen and the FF label for the second single, a cover of Dead Or Alive's Eighties-defining 'You Spin Me Round'. This became Single Of The Week in the now-defunct *Melody Maker*: other magazines proclaimed them the UK answer to Green Day.

Bemused by this adulation, Caffeine recruited Therapy? producer Harvey Birrell for the recording of a debut album, the cumbersomely-titled *What The Hell Am I Gonna Do When She Comes*, released in October 1998 and receiving rave reviews in the rock press. The third single, 'Kill The Brave', consolidated this success, but the ultimate sign that the band had risen to exalted heights came when the kings of Calipunk, the Offspring, invited them to open for them on their UK tour in early 1999. An unexpected bonus came when Offspring guitarist Noodles wore a Caffeine T-shirt on MTV. This was followed by tours with the old-school punks the Dickies.

All this smooth progress was bound to be hampered at some point, and sure enough Tony Marshall opted to depart in summer 1999. Since then the drum stool has been occupied by Pete Munro (ex-Speedurchin), Alan French and Andy

Clarke: the line-up may be more stable for a time, as the band record and promote their as-yet-untitled second album, also to be released on Fluffy Freako. With their currently high profile, it can surely be only a matter of time until a major label snaps them up.

KEITH CAPUTO

www.keithcaputo.com

When Life Of Agony split in 1999, singer Keith Caputo – always a reclusive, cerebral individual – signed a solo deal with Roadrunner. To date, his post-LOA career has consisted of one album, *Died Laughing*, of which he has said, "This record represents me going through my tragedies and understanding them to become the person that I'm becoming." Although nu-metal is too simple a term for Caputo's music, the ingredients are certainly all there: the riffs, the soul-searching, and the willingness to express emotions in music.

Life Of Agony specialised in skull-crushing riffing on the three studio albums they produced over eight years of activity (a live album and a best-of was released in 2000 – see separate entry), but towards the end of their career, Caputo felt that their music "wasn't what I was interested in saying musically, poetically or spiritually". Inspired by metaphysical studies, the singer embarked on his solo project in a more considered frame of mind than LOA's standard furious approach, recruiting non-metal session musicians such as Jeff Thall (Bryan Ferry, Ultravox) and Craig Ross (Lenny Kravitz). The result was an intelligent, varied and above all questioning album: high points included 'Cobain (Rainbow Deadhead)' – a eulogy to the Nirvana singer – the orchestral 'Home', and 'Brandy Duval', a homage to Caputo's mother, who died from an overdose while he was a child. Finally, Caputo made a successful attempt to cover Annie Lennox's 'Why', a sweeping ballad that stands perhaps as the most unlikely song ever to be covered by a metal singer.

Caputo activity has been thin on the ground since 1999. Possibly he is considering his next move: let us hope for his return.

CHARGER

www.undergroove.co.uk

Another young metal band expected to take up a prominent place at the vanguard of British nu-metal before too long is Charger, whose brutal combination of downtuned riffs and snarled vocals led Amen, among others, to request their presence for live support slots. Consisting of Tim (vocals), Jay (guitar), Jim (guitar), Tom (bass) and Paul (drums), the band were formed in the less-than-inspiring environment of Staffordshire in 1998 and recorded a demo, *Haulin' Ass*, to some local acclaim.

A track, 'Black Acid Rape', was chosen for the Lockjaw sampler *Helping You Back To Work Vol II*, and a West Midlands label, Undergroove, offered them a deal in early 1999. An EP, *Fuzzbastard* (no – me neither) was recorded and, after a tour with Raging Speedhorn and Tribute To Nothing, Charger released a debut album, *The Foul Year Of Our Lord,* in November 2000.

The departure of original bassist Jez proved to be no hindrance (the band played several gigs without a bass player until the arrival of new four-stringer Tom) and the Amen tour and slots with the Ross Robinson-produced Vex Red ensued. All the live activity helped to attract media attention to the band, which has also played with Brutal Deluxe, One Minute Silence and Defenestration.

CHIMAIRA

www.chimaira.com

Formed in 1998 by ex-Ascension guitarist Jason Hager, Chimaira (named after the mythical monster formed of several parts: an apt metaphor, Hager felt, for the six-piece band) comes from Cleveland, a city with an active hardcore and metal scene. Recruiting fellow hardcore-monger Rob Arnold (sometime Skipline axeman), singer Mark Hunter, bassist Jim LaMarca, drummer Andy Herrick and sampler/keyboard player Chris Spicuzza, the band embarked almost immediately on several American tours with big bands such as Machine Head, Cannibal Corpse, Six Feet Under, Snapcase, Will Haven, Candiria and Overkill, attracting a fanbase from the extreme metal scenes as well as their beloved punk background.

Scoring an indie deal with the East Coast Empire label and releasing an EP, *Painting The White To Grey*, Chimaira received some unexpected props from none other than Slipknot, who insisted that a DJ play the song 'Dead Inside' during a radio interview they were giving. The song remained on major-station playlists for several weeks and has been an extremely positive omen for the future.

CLAWFINGER: The first Scandinavian nu-metallers

CLAWFINGER

www.clawfinger.se

An influential Scandinavian band almost solely responsible for the first wave of European rap-metal, Clawfinger were formed in 1988 when four hospital workers (Jocke Skog, Zak Tell, Erlend Ottem and Bard Torstensson) found themselves stationed on the same ward in Rosenlunds Hospital in Stockholm. Noticing Zak's propensity to wander around the hospital corridors rapping to himself, Bard approached him with the idea of forming a band. The duo composed a song, 'Junkie Joe', and played it for Skog and Torstensson, who suggested ways of improving it.

A demo was the next logical step, and the newly-christened band retreated to Bard's apartment to record a cassette. Three songs were recorded: 'Profit Preacher', 'Waste Of Time' and the unequivocally-titled 'Nigger' (an anti-racism tirade, in case you were wondering). The tape went on to win Demo Of The Week on a Swedish radio station in the summer of 1992 and attracted the attention of the local MVG label, which signed them up in September of that year.

This unexpected good fortune led to a collaboration (and a successful single) with the now-disappeared Swedish rap act Just D, but much more was to come. A debut album, *Deaf Dumb Blind*, was released in the spring of 1993, charting in several countries and going on to sell an entirely unpredicted 600,000 units: Clawfinger supported the release by playing at most of the major European festivals and support slots with grunge stalwarts Alice In Chains and the old-school thrash metallers Anthrax.

1994 saw the band undertake a 55-date tour and win no fewer than four Zeppelin Awards and two Swedish Grammys. Clearly Clawfinger's patented aggressive, yet funky,

CLUTCH: Old-school nu-metallers

rap and riff style was to the Swedes' taste: this was demonstrated further by the impact of the follow-up album, *Use Your Brain*, released in 1995, which also went on to break the half-million barrier.

The ensuing years have seen Clawfinger remain popular in Europe (they regularly play huge venues, and their records sell extremely well) but remain little more than a club act in the UK and America. Why this should be so is not clear; perhaps their occasionally lightweight style has seen them left behind in those territories by heavier exponents of the rap-metal idiom. However, thanks to their willingness to

experiment (1997's self-titled album was more experimental than previous long-players – the lyrics of 'Two Sides' were in Arabic, and the bonus tracks were intended to allow the listener to remix a Clawfinger song), the band are unlikely to call it a day just yet.

CLUTCH

www.pro-rock.com

A Maryland quartet consisting of vocalist Neil Fallon, guitarist Tim Sult, bassist Dan Maines and drummer Jean Paul Gaster, Clutch were formed in 1991 and initially specialised in the early rapcore style of funk-metallers such as the Red Hot Chili Peppers but later mellowed out into a still-satisfying mainstream rock style. Their primary claim to fame is that they were offered a major record deal after a single demo track was released by an independent label.

In their decade of activity they have released four studio albums and a rarities collection, becoming in the process one of the old-school of nu-metal. A regular fixture on festivals and music TV, it appears that Clutch will remain of cult rather than widespread interest unless a chart single emerges to enthrall the MTV generation.

COAL CHAMBER

www.coalchamber.com

If seasoned observers of the nu-metal scene were asked to identify the most obviously 'gothic' band in the public eye, LA's Coal Chamber would probably be the first candidate. Predominantly dressed in black (none of your red Fred Durst baseball caps here, thank you very much), smeared with corpsepaint-like make-up and indulging in all the mascaraed, dry-iced clichés of the gothic genre, the Chamber stand out a mile from the hip-hop and funk-influenced end of metal. The more introspective of the world's teenage metalheads love them, of course, and their current position near the top of the nu-metal tree looks set to continue.

The band came together in 1994 when singer Dez Fafara and guitarist Miguel

COAL CHAMBER: They're just Goths

Rason (dubbed 'Meegs' by his friends) met after responding to an advert in a musicians' publication. A drummer, Mike Cox, and a bass player, Rayna Foss (recruited after a friend of hers informed her of the audition – this friend would later marry Fafara), were added to the line-up: all four musicians combined a love of dark theatrical gloom with the punk energy of the Pistols and the Stooges.

A self-produced demo tape, featuring 'Loco', which would become a signature

be in the offing (Coal Chamber had attracted heavyweight support from the likes of Fear Factory guitarist Dino Cazares and producer Ross Robinson) but all was not well. Before Coal Chamber could move to the next stage, however, Fafara had some issues to confront: his wife couldn't accept his commitment to the band and he left for almost six months. Ultimately, however, the lure of the music proved stronger than his marriage and the couple split in traumatic circumstances.

CRAZY TOWN: Do not feed this band

Chamber song, led to appearances at clubs such as the legendary Whiskey A Go-Go, and a buzz began to build around the band: Coal Chamber were lucky that Korn's angst-filled debut album had recently hit the Californian metal scene. A&R reps were scouring the scene for the next metal sensation, and the Chamber's expert combination of hardcore with enormous riffs proved to be just the ticket.

By mid-1994 a record deal appeared to

In late 1995 the demo tape was brought to Roadrunner. A deal was signed at Christmas and arrangements were made for a debut album to be recorded the following year. Two rookie producers (Jay Gordon, a musician, and Jay Baumgardner, an engineer at the local NRG studios) asked to be given the chance to hit the jackpot by producing a big album, and a self-titled debut album was duly laid down. Although the results were received positively, Fafara later described the recording process as 'pure hell', later explaining that, "The day I started recording my vocals, my wife left me. She left me in the driveway of my home, taking the dog and everything I fuckin' owned".

In a bizarre twist, it seems that Dez's wife asked him if he was 'all right' before she left. The singer was scheduled to record his vocals mere minutes later – and the chorus of the first track he recorded, "Do I seem alright to you?" was recorded in sheer anguish. The song remains a difficult listen, just as Slipknot's screamingly emotional 'Scissors' would be five years later.

The debut album and its successor, the less intense *Chamber Music*, sold in droves and the band have since attained a place in the upper echelons of nu-metal. A third long-player, tentatively entitled *Dark Days*, is expected in 2002: and as long as the masses enjoy a touch of make-up with their inner pain, the future of Coal Chamber will be assured.

COLD

http://coldmusic.com

A discovery of Limp Bizkit's Fred Durst, who comes from the same city (Jacksonville, Florida), Cold is less hip-hop-based than the Bizkit, preferring to delve into the bleak world of gothic atmospheres and electronic atmospheres. Durst heard of Cold's complex, pessimistic work and helped them to a deal with Flip Records, where he is an A&R scout, and nurtured them through the recording of a self-titled debut album in 1998 and a follow-up, the cathartic *13 Ways To Bleed On Stage*. Although they have built a cult following for their dexterous, innovative approach, the band has not yet achieved the heights to which its outspoken mentor has promised it can ascend.

CRAZY TOWN

www.crazytown.com

An in-your-face seven-man rap-rock outfit from Los Angeles, Crazy Town are among the purest hip-hop acts in this book: in fact, they barely scrape into the nu-metal arena, such is their dedication to all that is rappable. They do indulge in a certain amount of riffing, however, so they qualify.

The fearsomely-tattooed rappers and songwriters Shifty Shellshock and Epic Mazur first made rhymes together in 1994, when they performed as a duo, the Brimstone Sluggers. Both men had grown up listening to hip-hop and punk: Mazur had even honed his MC credentials by going to the same school as Ice Cube and Everlast of House Of Pain. The Sluggers recorded various demos (and appeared on records by other artists) but it wasn't until the recruitment of a full band – Faydoedeelay (bass), Rust Epique (guitar), Trouble Valli (guitar), DJ AM (turntables) and JBJ (drums) – that they felt ready to record a proper album.

The band's rising reputation on the Californian rock scene attracted no less a corporate behemoth than Columbia, which offered Crazy Town a deal. The debut album, *The Gift Of Game*, was produced by Orgy and Coal Chamber fader-tweaker Josh Abraham and Epic, and featured the rapping skills of KRS-One and Mad Lion. It was an instant success on both sides of the Atlantic thanks to the singles 'Butterfly', a mellow, whispering love song, and its polar opposite, 'Revolving Door' - a song about shagging any woman in sight. Come on – this is essentially a hip-hop band, after all: what did you expect?

CREASE

A lower-echelon act waiting for their big break, Crease were formed after years of slogging through a variety of hardcore bands in South Florida. Consisting of Kelly, Fritz, Greg and Eric, the band initially called themselves Excessive (or XSF, depending on who you believe) until the name Crease popped into a member's head one evening during a console-game session. An independent record deal (with a label which the band prefer not to name) fell through, leaving Crease frustrated and holding a pile of half-recorded songs.

However, perseverance won through and the band recorded an EP which gained some local airplay. The appropriately-titled song 'Frustration' became a radio hit, leading to a New York showcase gig, after which various labels stepped up and the future immediately started to look brighter. The question now is merely whether Crease can make good on their early promise. Watch this space.

CUBANATE

www.cubanate.com

Like Germany's Atari Teenage Riot a brutal mixture of guitars and industrial noise, Britain's Cubanate is the project of vocalist Marc Heal and guitarist Phil Barry, who recruit additional musicians as necessary. Also like the Ataris, Cubanate have a clearly-defined left-wing agenda, driven by Heal's experiences as a boy living in the Middle East ("I remember the complete poverty of the other kids," he has said, "[who] were crawling and dying in the dirt. And I grew up with it, so it seemed normal") and an early career as an advertising executive in London.

Having been introduced to the joys of industrial rock and techno, Heal joined forces with Barry and Graham Rayner (keyboards) and Steve Etheridge (percussion). Early gigs both as headliners and supporting Sheep On Drugs saw the crowd react with ferocious enthusiasm to Heal's frenzied performances, leading some excitable media types to describe him variously as a 'bulldog', a 'leather-clad psycho' and (best of all) a 'cornered rhino'.

An audience began to build up in Germany, where noisy, industrial techno has always been popular, and Cubanate signed to the Dynamica label, based in Berlin. A single, 'Bodyburn', was released as a variety of mixes (a notable retweak coming from sometime Nitzer Ebb mainstay Julian Beeston, who would go on to form a close relationship with the band) and received positive reviews. Rayner and Etheridge chose to leave Cubanate at this stage, but Heal and Barry were content to continue as a duo, with the occasional involvement of Beeston.

An album, *Antimatter*, appeared in September 1993, and was followed up by the *Metal* EP the following year. A UK tour with grindcore legends Carcass then attracted death threats after audiences came close to rioting: matters weren't helped by the national press, which wrote that Cubanate had "provoked an outbreak of demented carnage".

All this nonsense was exacerbated by an on-air row between Heal and Iron Maiden singer Bruce Dickinson on the *Radio 1 Rock Show* in January 1995. The cause of the argument is unclear, but it seems that the veteran metaller was so incensed that he gave out what he thought was the Cubanate singer's home telephone number on air. Threats flooded in, but the number was in fact wrong and the incident went down as one of the more surreal episodes in Cubanate's career. It certainly did no harm to sales of *Cyberia*, their second album.

A tour with Front Line Assembly followed, for which guitarist Shep Ashton and keyboard player Darren Bennett were employed, and another long-player, *Barbarossa*, appeared in April 1996. However, both Heal and Barry had begun to tire of the industrial-metal concept: Heal explained, "When the first Cubanate album came out... we were doing something that was absolutely brand new, that no-one had done before. But I freely admit that five years on, the idea of fusing guitars and techno together... is now kind of common currency". He was right, of course; the rise of Nine Inch Nails and Rammstein had made the clanking sounds of electro-metal almost predictable, and so album number three, 1998's *Interference* (released after a move to the TVT label), featured the sounds of drum'n'bass as well as a new overall texture. Fans responded positively, and the change of style was accepted as a beneficial development.

Since then Heal has worked with Pigface, performing vocals on their song 'Burundi', as well as forging a profitable musical alliance with Front 242 and Cobalt 60 composer Jean Luc DeMeyer. The two industrialists formed an ad hoc project called C-Tec and have worked on various soundtracks, including that of the Playstation game *Grand Turismo*. Cubanate themsleeves have continued to tour, with the help of the guitarist/keyboard player Dave Bianchi and guitarist Roddy Stone.

CYCLEFLY

www.cyclefly.com

The route from Cork to LA is not travelled often. But the world of nu-metal is an unpredictable place, and so when the five-piece Cyclefly, residents of the Irish village of Aghada, about four hours' drive from Dublin, were offered the chance to record an album in California, they took it and no-one thought twice.

Formed in 1995, Cyclefly comprises two Irishmen (singer Declan O'Shea and his brother Cieran), an Italian (Nono Presta) and two Frenchmen (Christian Montagne and Jean Michel Cavallo). The latter three had spent the early Nineties playing in a local band called Seventeen, and on its collapse in 1995 asked the O'Shea brothers if they would form a band with them. However, Declan and Cieran were flat broke and, having been offered the chance to take up employment at Eurodisney near Paris, declined the musicians' invitation. On a return trip home several months later, the five men met up for a jam – and such was the chemistry that the brothers decided to stay at home and try to make something of the band.

Adopting the name Cyclefly from the title of a painting that Declan had recently

CYCLEFLY: Nu-metal from the Emerald Isle

finished, the O'Sheas brought a powerful set of influences (Iggy Pop, The Ramones, Motörhead) to the band, as well as a serious commitment to the music – Cieran had once spent £1,000 on a round trip to London just to catch a show by the fabled industrial rockers Ministry. Local tours saw the CF sound refined to a peak of precision, which brought them to the attention of the Radioactive label.

The deal was struck and to their surprise, Cyclefly were asked to record a debut album with Skunk Anansie, Red Hot Chili Peppers and Tool producer Sylvia Massy in Los Angeles. Sessions commenced in early 1999 and the result, *Generation Sap*, was issued in the summer. A gig at the city's legendary Whisky A-Go-Go club on the Sunset Strip must have felt strange to the young Aghada emigrants, to say the least. Cyclefly remain one of the few nu-metal bands to emerge from Ireland, which has traditionally tended to contribute more to the rock and pop genres.

D

DEADLIGHTS
www.elektra.com

A band too new to warrant more description than a simple recommendation, Los Angeles' Deadlights are singer Duke, Billy Roan (guitar), Jerry Montano (bass) and Jim Falcone (drums) and have been compared with the cream of the West Coast's nu-metal movement such as Coal Chamber, Fear Factory and System Of A Down. The power and melodic content of their sound has led to the formation of a dedicated fanbase and, as and when national tours appear (step forward, Ozzy), a deal should be forthcoming.

DEFENESTRATION

Defenestration (which translates as 'chucking someone through a window' to me and you) is a much-hyped group of British teenagers, whose frenzied live shows supporting Brutal Deluxe, Raging Speedhorn and Napalm Death (whose singer Barney Greenaway signed them to his Dream Catcher label in 2000) have gained them grudging approval from many cynical observers. Their sole album to date, *One Inch God*, is a suitably aggressive piece of work and has ensured that a keen set of followers turns up at their shows.

The great youthful hope of British nu-metal? Perhaps. After all, the combination of youth and extreme energy did the trick for Raging Speedhorn.

DEFTONES

www.deftones.com

Clear contenders for the Limp Bizkit and Fear Factory crown, Deftones are one of the most innovative bands on the nu-metal scene and have consistently pushed out barriers across their six-year, three-album career – a fact recognised by no less a personage than Madonna, who signed them to her label, Maverick, in the States.

The band consists of vocalist Chino Moreno, guitarist Abe Cunningham, drummer Chi Cheng, bassist Frank Delgado and DJ Stephen Carpenter, who specialise in gritty, mid-tempo riffing with a sophisticated edge lacking in many of their contemporaries' work. America has bought into the Deftones' message with vigour and they are on the point of major international success. This development was made more likely in early 2001 when their third album, *White Pony*, netted them a Grammy ahead of Slipknot, Marilyn Manson and Pantera.

Formed in the early Nineties, the first Deftones album was 1995's *Adrenaline*, a simpler, rawer effort than their more recent work, but an invigorating listen nonetheless: headbangers bought it in droves and it was recognised as being among the very first albums to combine basic rap-rock with the smooth, scooped guitar sound that Fear Factory had made so popular. It went on to sell over 500,000 copies.

The same was true of *Around The Fur*, released two years later after solid touring had ratcheted up the band's profile still further. This time, however, there was evidence of a certain diversification: elements of new wave economy and even

DEFTONES: Pretenders to the nu-metal throne

the spiky gloom of goth could be heard. Two singles, 'Be Quiet And Drive (Far Away)' and 'My Own Summer (Shove It)', made the MTV A-list and allowed a new generation of listeners access to the 'Tones, while the album's inclusion of a Depeche Mode classic, 'To Have And To Hold', made the band one of the first to cover an Eighties standard – now a common nu-metal practice.

White Pony, released in 2000, is undoubtedly their best work to date: as Moreno says, "I'm better at fucking with your head now". This new-found versatility was complemented by the production work of Sepultura and Slipknot producer/remixer Terry Date, and a guest appearance by Tool singer Maynard James Keenan on 'Passenger' makes the song a fascinating duet and a high point of the album.

At the time of writing, the Deftones' crowd-pulling power is at a peak. Proof of this was seen in June 2001, when the band headlined a Limp Bizkit show in the UK when the Limps were forced to cancel – most of the crowd chose to stay on, despite having paid heavily for the right to see the Florida rap-metallers in action. No mean feat, and a good sign for the future.

DILUTRAL

www.splendid-monkey.freeserve.co.uk

Adhering to the small-town pattern of many of the angriest bands in this book, Dilutral (which sounds like a kind of bleach, unfortunately) come from the suburbs of Southampton and are made up of vocalist Kai Harris, guitarists J. Needham and Philip J. Harrison, bassist Dave Corney (who also handles keyboards and decks) and drummer Darran Gregory. What makes them stand out from the nu-rock crowd is their deft mixing of unexpected elements of ambient and trip-hop into their powerful sound, and their crafting of reportedly exquisite harmonies.

Formed in 1997, the band spent a couple of years knocking out strong but basic hardcore before opening up their sound to new influences with the recruitment of a new guitarist. The successful new approach meant that appearances with Raging Speedhorn, Sanctum and Lostprophets were met with enthusiasm by the provinces' nu-metal kids. A self-released mini-album, *Everything:*

DILUTRAL: Nu-kids on the block

Nothing, has led to a higher profile still.

What these young bands from out of London and the big cities have to their advantage is anger, bred by the unchanging passivity of their environments, which they interpret as conservatism and stagnancy. Many a Londoner would pay for a dose of the rage which fills bands like Dilutral: so catch them while they're still annoyed. Mind you, they may have to undergo a name-change first.

DISTURBED

www.disturbed1.com

At the forefront of nu-metal (they headlined the second stage at the 2001 UK Ozzfest), Chicago's Disturbed are an appropriately powerful outfit driven by the issues-laden personality of singer David Draiman. As with many other alt-metal frontmen (Korn's Jonathan Davis is a notable example), he lays much of the blame for his angst-filled lyrics at the door of his conservative parents, who foresaw the young Draiman's future as a teacher or salesman.

Dan Donegan (guitar), Mike Wengren (drums), and Fuzz (bass) had played together for some time, fruitlessly trying to recruit a singer, before the arrival of David in 1997, who also suggested the band's name. Building a fearsome live reputation on the south side of Chicago, Disturbed initally based their approach solely on the

DISTURBED: The laughing boys of nu-metal

standard monstrous riffing, but as time passed and the players' confidence grew, an electronic element was brought into the band's sound.

A much sought-after demo tape attracted the Giant label, who signed them and released an album, *The Sickness*, in early 2000. Disturbed remain one of nu-metal's brightest hopes.

DOG EAT DOG

www.dogeatdog.com

A band that embraces many different styles – including a trademark saxophone, often placed high in the mix – Dog Eat Dog were a popular touring band thoughout the Nineties, but have since been relegated to cult status as their quirky, lightweight style has slowly fallen out of fashion.

Dave Neabore and Sean Kilkenny had played with various New Jersey rock bands in the late Eighties, principally in Mucky Pup, who also numbered six-stringer Dan Nastasi in their line-up. Neabore and Kilkenny started writing songs together in 1990 after a long Mucky Pup tour: the other Pups decided that the direction they were pursuing was not for them, and so the duo continued alone. A singer, John Connor, was recruited, as well as a drummer named Brett – the first of many to occupy the drum stool.

After a debut gig in front of 50 toga-clad beer drinkers in Neabore's basement,

the still-unnamed band persuaded Nastasi to join them and played more shows under the dubious names of F-Troop, B-Load and Rubber Band. Two demos were successfully recorded, which featured artwork by the professional skateboarder Andy Howell (whose 'doghouse' logo led to the name Dog Eat Dog) and with which a useful contact – Billy Graziadei of fellow New Yorkers Biohazard – was sufficiently impressed to recommend the band to Roadrunner. A deal was duly signed and an EP, *Warrant*, was recorded and released.

Tours with reggae-hardcore outfit Bad Brains ensued, which led to the appearance of BB singer Daryl Jenifer on the first Dog Eat Dog album, *All Boro Kings*. Thanks to a European tour with Biohazard, the album quickly sold over half a million units, although all was not running smoothly: Nastasi bowed out of touring, pleading family commitments, and Cro-Mags axeman Parris Mayhew stepped in, to be replaced in turn by Marc DeBacker.

In late 1995 DED were awarded Breakthrough Artist of The Year at MTV's European Music Awards, much to their surprise – even beating the planet-straddling Alanis Morissette to the gong, presented by the late Michael Hutchence. This turn of events proved to be the highest point of the band's career to date. Later work featured cameo appearances from none other than Ronnie James Dio (the band had joked that one song was so heavy, only Dio could sing it – and just for kicks, contacted his management) and

Wu-Tang Clan producer RZA. Although successful tours with Metallica, Kiss, Rage Against The Machine, No Doubt and Sepultura kept the DED flag flying, it was clear that a rethink was necessary. However, they have legions of loyal fans, and a new Dog Eat Dog project is said to be on the cards.

DOGTOFFEE

www.dogtoffee.co.uk

A relatively obscure nu-metal outfit that has toured with bands of the calibre of Electric Frankenstein, the Damned, DOA, Sloppy Seconds, B-Movie Rats, King Prawn, the Dwarves, Therapy? and New Bomb Turks, Dogtoffee were first formed in 1996 in Manchester, England by vocalist/guitarist Bobby Heavenly with bassist Kid Fury, guitarist the Hammer and drummer Satan G. Early rehearsals took place in the local Catholic church but stopped abruptly when the clergy discovered the 'earthy' nature of their songs.

Various labels have committed to issuing Dogtoffee recordings, but the band's main strength appears to be as a live act, despite the replacement of Satan G with a more sedate sticksman.

DOWNER

www.downermusic.com

The Orange County, California-based four-piece Downer spent many years on the edges of the nu-metal and hardcore punk scenes, with success always just eluding them: in more reflective moments, the members – John Scott (vocals), Aaron Silberman (guitar), Jed Hathaway (bass) and Tracey Sledge (drums) – acknowledge that perhaps it was their choice of name that turned fate against them. Their latest album, a self-titled effort recorded with Black Sabbath/Alice Cooper producer Bob Marlette, may be the one to do the trick.

The core of Downer is Scott and Silberman, who grew up listening to local hardcore acts such as Inside Out (which featured future Rage Against the Machine frontman Zack de la Rocha) and the young Offspring, for whom they opened in a pizza restaurant shortly after forming Downer. Scott had honed his impassioned vocal style with Headfirst and Silberman had refined his axemanship in Mission Impossible: both bands have since disappeared into oblivion, but the talents both musicians took from the experience were developed enough for Downer to become a sophisticated, unpredictable act.

DOG EAT DOG: Barking up the nu-metal tree

However, only the small Ammunition label recognised Downer as having anything to offer the world, and released a self-titled EP and a 1997 album, *Wrestling With Jesus*. Protracted touring with Earth Crisis and on the Lollapalooza tour meant that they saw many bands rise past them (their second gig had featured some support act by the unlikely name of Korn). However, the powerful live shows brought Downer to the attention of Roadrunner at last, who signed them up in 1998 and arranged for the Marlette sessions. Although the album – you guessed it: *Downer* – was received with moderate praise, the band have yet to rise above the status of dependable C-league metal act. Perhaps this will have to suffice.

DROWNING POOL

www.drowningpool.com

Taking their name from the 1975 Paul Newman film shortly after their formation in the mid-Nineties, Dallas' Drowning Pool is made up of singer Dave Williams, guitarist CJ Pierce, bassist Stevie Benton and drummer Mike Luce. Recording a demo EP, *Pieces Of Nothing*, the band began to play local gigs and were soon invited on tour by the nu-metal outfit Sevendust.

Successful live dates with Kittie and Hed(pe) followed, but a record deal didn't come Drowning Pool's way until a second recording entered the Top 10 of the local KEGL radio station.

The Wind Up label was the first to secure the DP collective signature and their debut album, *Sinner*, appeared in June 2001. Produced by Orgy/Godsmack/Papa Roach knob-twiddler Jay Baumgardner, the album was received with approval by critics and fans and led to a slot on the Ozzfest. Whether they can capitalise on this early success – remember, the band have only been touring at the top level for a year – remains to be seen.

DRY KILL LOGIC

www.drykilllogic.com

Situated somewhere between the gothic iciness of Coal Chamber and the hardcore riffing of Biohazard, Dry Kill Logic takes its influences from the old school, namechecking artists as established as King Diamond, Pantera and Sepultura while acknowledging a certain debt to the arty electronica of Tool and Fear Factory.

Formed in Westchester, New York in 1995, Cliff Rigano (vocals), Scott Thompson (guitar), Dave Kowatch (bass) and Phil Arcuri (drums) set up a label, Psychodrama, and released an EP, *Cause Moshing Is Good Fun*, two years later. Filling support slots with thrash and punk acts such as Flotsam And Jetsam, Exodus and Pro-Pain, the band began to gain a local following and was offered a deal by Roadrunner.

The first album, *Elemental Evil*, was recorded with Overkill/Rakim producer Andy Katz in July 1998 and was duly promoted with shows opening for System Of A Down, Anthrax, Incubus and the Misfits, before exhaustion dictated that the band take a break.

1999 proved to be a pause for thought, but new material was written by the start of 2000 and went on to become the second album, *The Darker Side Of Nonsense*. A tougher, more surreal record than the debut, the album was still selling well at the time of writing.

EARTH CRISIS

www.earthcrisis.cc

One of the more politically outspoken bands in this book (only Amen and Rage Against The Machine are more vociferous), Earth Crisis both practise and preach a straight-edge lifestyle. For those not in the know, this is a fearsomely-dedicated abstinence from drugs, alcohol, nicotine, all animal products including meat, and in extreme cases even caffeine and prescription drugs such as aspirin. The regime requires significant inner strength and, in Earth Crisis's case, forms a central mainstay of the band's lyrics.

The members – singer Karl Buechner, guitarists Scott Crause and Eric Edwards, bassist Bulldog and drummer Dennis Merrick – first came together in Syracuse in New York in 1989. Buechner was a mere

18 years old at the time, but this didn't stop the band signing to the local Conviction label and releasing a strong hardcore punk-metal debut, *All Out War*, which led to a move to the bigger (but still indie) Victory company.

The Victory album, *Destroy All Machines*, appeared in 1995 and was reissued as *Firestorm* a year later. The buzz surrounding the band, whose political sloganeering encompassed a variety of left-wing issues, was such that features on Earth Crisis appeared on national TV and in the *New York Times*. The follow-up, the apocalyptically-named *Gomorrah's Season Ends*, was successful enough to secure the band a slot on the first Ozzfest in 1997, and their profile was bolstered further by a sold-out show with labelmates Strife and Snapcase at LA's Whisky A-Go-Go, which was recorded for a video, *The California Takeover... Live*.

After a rarities collection, *The Oath That Keeps Me Free* (1998), Earth Crisis wanted to move to a more far-reaching platform and accepted an offer from Roadrunner, who released *Breed The Killers* the same year. They then toured with RR acts Fear Factory and Sepultura. However, for reasons still undisclosed, band and label parted

company shortly after and EC returned to Victory, which has since issued two more albums, *Slither* (2000) and *Last Of The Sane* (2001).

Buechner, a persuasive speaker, has appeared at various public gatherings, including a speech before Congress. Clearly he has outgrown his anarcho-punk roots – can you imagine John Lydon addressing the US government? Perhaps it's best not to try.

EARTHTONE9

www.earthtone9.co.uk

A British band that has moved from what we traditionally think of as nu-metal (some rapping and hip-hop elements, big beats, scooped guitars) on its earlier releases to a genuinely innovative approach, Earthtone9's current line-up is Karl Middleton (vocals), Owen Packard (guitar), Joe Roberts (guitar), Dave Anderson (bass) and Simon Hutchby (drums). Owen and Joe had previously played in a band called Blastcage and had toured with the UK thrash metal band Gomorrah, which split shortly after.

EARTHTONE 9: Innovative UK scene-stealers

excitement (or even response), the band turned to a friend and ex-member of Gomorrah, Jose Griffin, who formed Copro Records, now a flourishing distribution company. Copro gathered the three tapes onto one CD in 1998 and called it *Lo-Definition Discord*. The album's influences – Tool, Helmet, Alice In Chains and many others – made it a satisfying blend of melody and power (the press have since called it 'art-rock') and Copro requested a second recording. This was *Off-Kilter Enhancement*, a record released in June 1999 which honed the ET9 style into what Karl described as "Tool on crack – we've got the dynamics of Korn and Deftones, but we're more heavy and grooving". Tours with One Minute Silence, combined with positive reviews from the rock press, proved sufficient to give the album a boost and despite one or two personnel shuffles at this point, public interest remained high.

Since then the Earthtone tale has been one of constant rise: the *Hi-Point* EP and the very accomplished *Arc'Tan'Gent* album of 2000 were hailed as masterpieces by normally sober rock critics, and their ascendance has been confirmed by tours with Soulfly and their own Evolution shows, which included high-quality acts such as Stampin' Ground.

FAKE

www.fakemusic.co.uk

One of the more promising modern metal bands to emerge from the UK to date (they accept the term 'nu-metal' – in fact, they started life as a plain rap-metal band – but prefer to label themselves 'hardcore-metal', because they can play fast, heavy, melodic or dark), Fake, from North Yorkshire, have garnered a certain amount of critical success.

Consisting of Sean Slinger (vocals), Jamie Stead (guitar, samples), David Green (bass) and Richard Hardy (drums), the band first recorded together in 1999, producing the uncompromising *Live It Like This* demo. An EP, *Failure Breeds Within The Minds Of*

The Weak, was released a year later and received great acclaim in the press. However, Fake split in late 2001, although a new incarnation is merely a matter of time. Remember where you read it first: bands like this don't come along very often.

FANTOMAS

FAKE: They burned brightly but briefly

www.ipecac.com/fantomas.php

A man with enormous vision and the perseverance to carry his ideas through, ex-Faith No More singer Mike Patton always exercised his weirder tendencies alongside FNM's distinguished career with his Mr. Bungle side-project, a metallic jazz hybrid. After his main band finally parted company in 1998, Patton wasted no time in taking Mr. Bungle's weird brand of songwriting to another level and launched a new project, the sporadically-active Fantomas. He also founded the eccentric Ipecac label.

Together with Melvins guitarist Buzz Osbourne, bass player Trevor Dunn (also of Bungle) and the legendary thrash metal drummer Dave Lombardo (Slayer, Testament, Grip Inc.), Patton's new band made a demo tape in 1998 and an eponymous album the following year. One of those bands that attracts enormous interest and critical praise – but sells hardly any records – Fantomas (named after a French literary anti-hero) played in several countries before producing a follow-up, *Director's Cut*, in 2001. Most fans don't quite understand what Patton is doing, but he remains a very welcome force for change anyway.

FEAR FACTORY

www.fearfactoryfanclub.com

Almost unique in the world of nu-metal for their willingness to push out the musical envelope and the scope of their vision (only Tool is their equal in terms of imagination), Los Angeles' Fear Factory were formed in 1990 as a pure death metal band by ex-Hateface singer Burton C. Bell, with drummer Raymond Herrera and guitarist Dino Cazares. After the band contributed tracks to a local metal compilation, Roadrunner (still an extreme label back then – death and thrash metal bands such as Deicide and Malevolent Creation were its mainstays) offered them a deal, which led to the recruitment of bassist

of their notoriously hardcore death metal audience, Fear Factory were praised for their vision and expectations began to build for a second album.

This came in the shape of *Demanufacture*, the first FF long-player to concern itself with technology and humanity (a prevailing Factory theme), and featured the talents of new bass player Christian Olde Wolbers. Not really a death metal album other than in some of its textures, the album was one of the first to qualify as 'nu-metal' on the strength of its diversity and bleak, oppressive atmosphere. It too was remixed, and the material it contained (rejigged by a whole host of remixers, including one or two dance music producers) was released as *Remanufacture (Cloning Technology),* in 1997.

FEAR FACTORY: Among the world's most experimental electronic metal bands

Andrew Shives and the release of an album, *Soul Of A New Machine*, in 1992.

Bell's guttural roar and Cazares' deep, visceral guitar parts made Fear Factory immediately popular, but what made them different from the hordes of other Californian metallers was their interest in remixing their work: some songs from *SOANM* were retweaked by the noted Front Line Assembly members Rhys Fulber and Bill Leeb and issued on an EP, *Fear Is The Mind Killer* (a quote from Frank Herbert's *Dune* novel) in 1993. Although the move might well have alienated many

Fear Factory's place in nu-metal was assured at this stage, and the two albums that have followed – *Obsolete* (1999) and *Digimortal* (2001) – have taken the electronic-metal combination and the concept of man's battle with technology to their logical limit. Next time around, the band may well have exhausted this particular seam: however, their energy certainly shows no signs of abating, as the Cazares/Herrera death metal side-project Brujeria, Cazares' collaboration with Soulfly's Max Cavalera as Nailbomb and Bell's G/Z/R testify.

FINGER ELEVEN

www.fingereleven.com

A Canadian alternative metal band that consists of Scott Anderson (vocals), James Black (guitar), Rick Jackett (guitar), Sean Anderson (bass) and Rich Beddoe (drums), Finger Eleven have gained a significant fan base since the release of their debut album, *Tip*, in 1997. Label difficulties left the band floundering a little in the late Nineties, but with the help of their loyal following Finger Eleven were able to regroup and set up another deal.

The result, 2001's *The Greyest Of Blue Skies*, was a gloomy, introspective record – reflecting the tribulations that the band had endured – but was welcomed by the FE fans, who continue to keep sales buoyant. A standout track on *The Greyest Of Blue Skies* is a reworking of Depeche Mode's 'Walking In My Shoes', a song which the band had played live for some years: more than just the standard Eighties cover which so many bands seem to feel is *de rigueur*, both fans and band feel that the song has developed a special meaning to them, and it remains a live high point.

40 BELOW SUMMER

www.40belowsummer.com

Taking their name from the concept of opposites – which also permeates the nice/nasty textures of their music – 40 Below Summer are a New Jersey-based metal band consisting of singer Max Illidge, guitarists Joe D'Amico and Jordan Plingos, bass player Hector Graziani and drummer Carlos Aguilar. The band first formed in 1998 when the Peru-born Aguilar – who had started his drum training by beating a pair of chopsticks on the back of a sofa – became friends with Illidge while playing in a band called Alien. The latter had been an actor since the tender age of twelve, when he had appeared in Broadway plays and (more impressively) as a child in Talking Heads' 'Burning Down The House' video.

After getting together with D'Amico, Graziani and Plingos, the band began gigging in New Jersey and New York and

FUNGER ELEVEN: At the top of the Canadian metal tree

recorded and self-released an album, *Sideshow Freaks*. This somehow got as far as the influential No Name Management company, which boasts Fear Factory and Slipknot on its roster, and a deal was struck. The newly-backed band played several showcase gigs nationwide, ultimately signing to the London label and recording an album, *Invitation To The Dance*, with the renowned producer Garth Richardson. The record was a success on the East Coast metal scene and it's clear that the first step for 40 Below Summer has been successfully negotiated.

FUDGE TUNNEL

www.linear-recording.com

Sharing the punk roots of late-Eighties bands such as Napalm Death and Extreme Noise Terror, Fudge Tunnel became a respected noisecore trio, consisting of Alex Newport (vocals/guitar), David Ryley (bass) and Adrian Parkin (drums). Formed in 1989, they shared their home town with the label that would ultimately sign them: Earache, home to many a grindcore and industrial-metal act.

1990 saw the release of the excellently-titled 'Sex Mammoth' single, immediately labelled Single Of The Year by the ferociously pro-indie NME. Earache then issued a debut album, *Hate Songs In E Minor*, which grabbed the headlines due to its cover art, a sketch of a decapitated man. The Nottingham Vice Squad seized early copies and a new cover was designed. Funnily enough, Earache had experienced something similar a couple of years before, when the police had reacted negatively to the artwork of Carcass' *Reek Of Putrefaction* – some people never learn, eh?

A 1992 EP entitled *Teeth* brought accusations that Fudge Tunnel had 'gone grunge' – an idea that was quickly refuted by the band. The topic was dismissed when the next album, 1993's *Creep Diets*, appeared: it was a melodic, heavy album, even containing acoustic touches, and light-years away from the fast-fading Seattle sound. The year was mostly spent on the road (Newport was also involved in the Max Cavalera project Nailbomb) and subsequent albums - *The Complicated Futility Of Ignorance* (1994) and *In A Word* (1995) saw the Tunnel remain at a steady level, neither gaining nor losing popularity.

FURY OF FIVE

www.victoryrecords.com/furyoffive.html

A hardcore band in every way except that their inventive knack with a riff has also attracted a significant set of followers from the metal scene, New Jersey's Fury Of Five have carved out a dedicated niche on the New York extreme club circuit and consists of James (vocals), Jay (guitar), Chico (guitar), Mike (bass) and Chris (drums).

Formed back in 1994, both band and fans seem to relish their long-standing underground status, although the Fury have released two singles, two albums (*No Time to Smile* and *At War With The World*) and have showed up on various compilation albums – the accepted medium through which most East Coast punk and metal outfits get their early exposure.

Will Fury Of Five always be an underground act? The answer was always assumed to be yes until recently, when the popularity of hardcore took off. All bets are off, so keep an eye out.

FUDGE TUNNEL: Too hardcore to last forever

G

GENITORTURERS

www.genitorturers.com

Many metal bands, including Marilyn Manson, Orgy and even Limp Bizkit, make a point of hinting coyly at the pleasures of kinky sex in their songs. Why not? It's rock'n'roll, after all. But most people's liberal shrugs become rather uncertain when they're faced with the barrage of whipping, piercing (nipples and genitals), sado-masochism, spanking, masturbation and general all-round nudity involved in a show by Florida's Genitorturers, who even take their name from a particularly excruciating sexual practice. The band has even gathered a loyal following, the Genheads, who regularly get into a froth of excitement when tickets for the annual 'Evening Of Torture' are auctioned off on the internet, paying high prices for the chance of a session with the band.

Led by the blonde singer Gen, a real-life dominatrix who includes the Marquis de Sade among her heroes, the band also includes guitarist Chains, keyboard player V. Stilletto, drummer Racci Shay and – most famously – Gen's husband, ex-Morbid Angel singer and bassist David Vincent, who abandoned the world's most successful death metal band to join this outfit under the stage name of Evil D. Presumably he thought the Genitorturers – themselves a death metal band when they formed in 1990 – would rise to greater things.

The Genitorturers were founded when a film company needed a sex-based stage show for an upcoming movie in the early Nineties. Attracted by Gen – who also works both as a professional body-piercer and as an organ reclamation technician in a local hospital, which is nice – the company signed the band up. The filming never took place, but the IRS label had been paying attention and offered the Genitorturers a contract. An album, *120 Days Of Genitorture*, was released in 1993, leading to a national tour, several dozen colourful tabloid headlines and a video, *Society Of Genitorture*, released in 1997 by – yes – G-Spot Films.

Subsequent albums have done moderately well on a cult level: 1998's *Sin City* and 2000's *Machine Love*, released by the Cleopatra label, have kept the torture levels healthy. A cover of the Divinyls' best-forgotten 'I Touch Myself' was a minor hit, and Gen was the subject of a supposedly autobiographical film, *Preaching To The Perverted*, in the late Nineties.

And the music? Industrial-tinged alternative metal, although that's probably irrelevant.

GENITORTURERS: Don't say we didn't warn you...

GLASSJAW

www.glassjawband.com

Another Ross Robinson discovery, Glassjaw have come a long way in a short time, with their first album, 2000's *Everything You Ever Wanted To Know About Silence*, already one of the more prominent stars in the glittering I Am galaxy. Vocalist Daryl Palumbo and guitarist Justin Beck first began making disorganised, organic music together in 1995 in the Long Island community where they grew up. Palumbo spent many years receiving treatment for Crohn's disease, an intestinal disorder that makes his life difficult to this day, but which has informed his lyrics with a certain insight: the music of Glassjaw is also a multifaceted affair, with Radiohead comparisons not uncommon.

Glassjaw's first work as a band didn't add up to much (the duo described themselves as "dorky looking" as teenagers), but with the later addition of Todd Weinstock (guitar), Manuel Carrero (bass) and Larry Gorman (drums), a much more focused outfit emerged, recording a demo which eventually found its way to Robinson. From then on, it was remarkably easy – as Beck tells it: "Ross showed up at a practice. We start a song. Ross stands up, waving his hands, and says, 'It's over, it's done. I want to do this, you've got a deal!' he told us. We couldn't believe it, and actually didn't believe it for weeks."

Robinson was serious, referring the band as "the new post-millennial destroyers of Adidas rock", and booking them into his preferred recording venue, Indigo Ranch in the LA suburb of Malibu. He also taught them to look deep into the music they had written for its true relevance, at one point stopping the sniggering band during a song and sobering them up with a few well-chosen words. The results, however, were pretty spectacular: the album contained standard riffing, plaintive pop melodies and several crushing sections aimed directly at the moshpit. Refreshingly, Palumbo claims that all the lyrics were inspired by Godzilla movies – it seems that Robinson didn't manage to block out the Glassjaw sense of humour after all.

Tours with acts such as Soulfly cemented the Glassjaw profile and, it seems, the future is theirs to do with as they wish.

GODHEAD: Where *do* they all come from?

GODHEAD

www.godhead.com

Although the Washington DC-based Godhead might seem to be just another set of fresh-from-school nu-metal hopefuls, they have in fact worked long and hard to get where they today – which is to say, signed to Marilyn Manson's Posthuman label, with a debut album, the gloomily-titled *2000 Years Of Human Error*, released in early 2001.

Like Fear Factory before them, Godhead have successfully broken several sets of metal rules by basing their sound on a combination of uncompromising riffing and a heavy reliance on electronics. To this end, the well-known Black Grape/U2/ Black Sabbath producer Danny Saber was drafted in to produce the album, while the mixing skills of John X Volaitis (previously flipping faders for Orgy, Korn and the 'God Of Fuck' himself, Manson) added a definite flair to the sound.

Forming in 1995 and gathering a local Washington fanbase thanks to support slots on tours by death metal joke band GWAR, eccentric goth-mongers Christian Death and the Genitorturers, Godhead released no fewer than three full-length albums on independent labels: *Godhead* (1994), *Nothingness* (1996) and *Power Tool Stigmata* (1998).

The band (vocalist Jason Miller, bassist/programmer The Method, guitarist Mike Miller and drummer James O'Connor) combined their unique sound – driving, layered percussion and bass with atmospheric guitars and impassioned vocals – with some vintage influences: primarily

GODSMACK

www.godsmack.com

Another gothically industrial band that has perfected its act across years of toil while waiting for society to take notice is Boston's Godsmack, featuring the Wiccan devotee Sully Erna (vocals), Tony Rombola (guitar), Robbie Merrill (bass) and Tommy Stewart (drums).

GODSMACK: Finally at the top

David Bowie, whose 1996 *Earthling* album was a Godhead favourite. The resulting clean, powerful approach comes to the fore on their cover of the Beatles' 'Eleanor Rigby', a version stripped of its original pathos and injected with the shiniest of modern-day sounds. The album was executive-produced by Marilyn Manson, with help from long-time Bowie collaborator and guitarist Reeves Gabrels. "In a way," says Miller of Manson, "we both come from the same place – underground industrial goth rock. But obviously he's somewhere else now, and he's trying to bring us up there!" It remains to be seen if an industrial take on a Sixties classic is the right recipe – but odd things do happen in the nu-metal world...

First formed in 1995, the band recorded an album, *All Wound Up*, for a paltry $2,500, and saw it achieve considerable local success of the back of radio airplay. The Republic label soon stepped in, signed them up, added some bonus tracks to *AWU* and reissued it as *Godsmack* – a seemingly instantaneous step into the big time. However, as Erna points out: "People seem to think we made it so big so quickly, but they should see it from our eyes. We went through years of flyering cars, selling CDs out of our trunks, booking the band ourselves, playing in front of 20 people on the road. When you're out there doing that, it seems like forever."

Godsmack went on to hit triple platinum in America, largely because four consecutive singles – 'Whatever' (not the

Oasis tune), 'Keep Away', 'Voodoo' and
'Bad Religion' - spent hundreds of weeks
on the charts between them. Clearly
something was good about the 'Smack
approach, and metal fans worldwide were
keen to hear more.

   Awake was a successful follow-up, and
combined with Godsmack's memorable
appearances on the Ozzfest 1999 and 2000
bills, meant that the band's profile was at
its apogee at the time of writing. As yet no
complaints have been received about the
potentially blasphemous nature of the
band's name – but it's got to happen
sometime, eh?

GUANO APES

www.guanoapes.com

The nearest thing that Germany has to
chart-metal, Guano Apes knock out
a reliable brand of angst-laden rap-rock and
have seen significant success in the
skate/snowboard community thanks to a
1998 single, 'Lord Of The Boards', which
became the theme tune for the 1998
European Snowboarding Championships.

   From Göttingen, the four-piece
(vocalist Sandra Nasic, guitarist Henning
Ruemenapp, bassist Stefan Ude and
drummer Dennis Poschwatta) were formed
in 1994 and scored a lucky break by
winning a national battle-of-the-bands-type
competition two years later. The
tournament, labelled *Local Heroes* and
sponsored by the European Viva TV
channel (a sort of Teutonic MTV),
saw the Apes win out over more than
1000 other entrants.

   The band's first single, 'Open Your
Eyes', was released by Gun later that
year and entered the Top 10,
remaining on the chart for the next six
months. This success was bolstered by
the Snowboarding Championships
tune: an album, *Proud Like A God*, was
released in Europe in 1997 and in
America two years later. At the time of
writing, the Guano Apes were touring
constantly and continuing to enjoy
music-TV exposure.

**GUANO APES: Angst-ridden Teutonic
met – on ice!**

H-BLOCKZ

Germany is well-known for its metal
bands. However, these have never
really been classifiable as nu-metal, perhaps
because of the population's evident thirst
for musical extremity: power metal was
invented there by the natives Helloween,
and Eighties thrash was headed up in
Europe by Kreator, Sodom and
Destruction, the unholy trinity of Teutonic
speed metal. Today most of the country's
metallic vanguard consists of retro acts
such as Hammerfall and Primal Fear, who
specialise in keeping the spirit of True
Metal alive – well, someone's got to do it.

   Other than by the Guano Apes
(see opposite), modern rap-inflected rock
has been practised only by
one major German
band, Münster's
H-Blockz,
named
for

no apparent reason after the Northern Irish political prisons. The band was formed in 1990 by vocalist Henning Wehland, together with guitarist Tim Tenambergen, bassist Stefan Hinz and drummer Johann-Cristoph Maass. After a few gigs at which their naive blend of Faith No More whimsy and the odd riff was received with moderate enthusiasm, a rapper, David Gappa, was added to the line-up and the familiar rap-rock sound was achieved as a result.

A deal with Berlin's Sing Sing Records followed in 1993 and an independent hit was notched up with 'Rising High', a rap-rock standard which remains a club and live staple. A fan base began to gather, inspired by the overseas racket of the brand-new Rage Against The Machine and keen to support any native crossover talent. An album, *Time To Move*, appeared the following year and immediately gained maximum exposure on the German Viva

helped bolster the band's following, as did another single, 'How Do You Feel?'. Greater success was to come with the release of the second album, *Discover My Soul*, issued in September 1996 to impressive reviews. Its crisp guitar sound and anthemic choruses made it ideal for radio airplay and once again, H-Blockz' appearances on the live circuit were a year-round highlight.

Since then the band have remained at a fairly constant level, a big fish on the central European nu-metal scene, where they were pioneers, but a club act in America. Slots on the Vans Warped Tour, songs on the soundtrack of the German cult film *Bang Boom Bang* and Henning's part-time job as a Viva presenter have all kept the band in the public eye. They are currently trying to break America with tours and the reissue of some of their recordings there, but chances are slim: however, they retain an intensely loyal Old World following.

HED (PE): Scissors, paper or stone?

music TV channel and European MTV. To capitalise on the album's success, 'Rising High' was reissued and once more sold well.

Festival slots at the German mega-show Rock Am Ring followed and *Time To Move* rapidly went gold in Germany and surrounding territories. MTV awarded H-Blockz a 'Local Hero' award, which

HED (PE)

www.hedpe.com

One of the most promising of the nu-metal new school, Hed (Pe) – thought to be based on Head Planet Earth, although this has never been confirmed or denied by the band themselves – are based on the intimidating vocals and stage presence of Paulo Sergio (also known as Jahred but usually referred to as MCUD). Born of Brazilian parents and raised in Huntington Beach, California (the origin of many punk and metal bands, notably Slayer), the frontman makes an instantly recognisable figure, sporting long dreadlocks which usually conceal his eyes.

The band were formed in 1994 when MCUD and Westyle (guitar) became friends on the Orange County hardcore scene. Recruiting guitarist Chizad, bassist Mawk, drummer BC and DJ Product, Hed (Pe) built a live following based on the powerful shows they performed at local venues such as the infamous Club 369. After the recording and self-release of an EP, *Church Of Realities*, it wasn't long before the Jive label stepped in to sign them.

1997 saw the release of a self-titled debut album and tours with heavyweights such as Korn, Slipknot and Kid Rock. A second long-player, *Broke*, released in 2000, was a more imaginative record, straying away from the rap-rock template towards classic rock sounds and world influences. It featured guest spots from System Of A Down vocalist Serj Tankian and Morgan Lander of all-girl metallers Kittie, and the band returned the favour by appearing on various other projects – MCUD on a Primer 55 album, DJ Product in a song by ex-Mötley Crüe drummer Tommy Lee's Methods Of Mayhem, and both musicians on the Lynn Strait tribute album, *Strait Up*. Hed (Pe) also covered Black Sabbath's 'Sabbra Cadabra' for a Sabs covers project released in 2000. A spot on the 2001 Ozzfest kept the flag flying.

HELMET

www.helmet.org

One of the first bands to depart from standard metal roots and evolve a new direction, Helmet have never enjoyed sustained commercial success thanks to their almost wilful eclecticism, but can bask in the respect of almost every nu-metal band thanks to their pioneering status. Focused on the guitar skills of ex-Band Of Susans player Page Hamilton – who famously trained as a jazz player – the band's riff-heavy approach is currently complemented by second guitarist Chris Traynor (sometime of Orange 9mm) as well as Henry Bogdan (bass) and John Stanier (drums).

The band started life in New York in 1989, kicking off some predictable controversy among America's parents with their todger-based moniker, and recorded an album, *Strap It On*, for a local independent label. Its success was a surprise to all concerned and led to a bidding war, which Interscope eventually won by offering Helmet an unusually cash-heavy deal. But it was the major-label debut, *Meantime* (no knob jokes here), which took the band into the big time: metal fans keen on grunge, Faith No More and the nascent rap-metal scene bought it by the truckload.

1994's oddly-titled follow-up *Betty* alienated one or two fans due to its shift into lighter, more thoughtful territory, but this was to be expected and the mostly loyal fanbase remained intact. It seemed that Helmet might rise to the level of rap-metal behemoths such as Rage Against The

HELMET: Imaginative players who pushed out the metal envelope

Machine, but by 1997's *Aftertaste* times had changed and pundits predicted that Helmet would remain at a cult level. The band's plateauing in sales over the ensuing years have proven this to be the case – although they've never had a real flop yet...

HUMAN WASTE PROJECT

Centring on the charismatic Aimee Echo, Huntingdon Beach's Human Waste Project was formed when bassist Jeff Schartoff and drummer Scott Ellis asked their friend Echo if she would join their band during a car ride to Lollapalooza. Guitarist John Monte was soon recruited, but was ousted in favour of the New York-born Mike Tempesta.

After scoring independent college-radio hits and touring with influential nu-metallers such as Deftones, Helmet and Korn, the band came to the attention of Ross Robinson, who produced their first album, *Electralux*, after a deal was struck with the Hollywood label. This was almost upset by both record company problems and the Malibu brush fires of 1996 – the band were obliged to pack up their equipment and evacuate the studio at one point – but in the end the album was released in late 1997.

The record was a moderate success, but Echo had become unhappy with the HWP line-up and departed to form two solo outfits, first Hero and then a band called Thestart. At the time of writing she is out of the public eye, although she remains a darling of the metal press.

HUMAN WASTE PROJECT: Aimee Echo – fingerlickin' good

HUNDRED REASONS

www.hundredreasons.com

A hotly-tipped UK nu-metal quintet with obvious punk influences, Hundred Reasons have been a popular live act to catch since their first single, 'Cerebra', came out in 1998. Aided by a *Kerrang!* award, the band – led by singer Colin Doran, whose enormous Afro immediately singles him out from nu-metal's standard baseball-capped skinhead look – have toured with indie-rock stalwarts such as Idlewild, but have yet to make any serious impact. However, the onstage antics of guitarists Larry Hibbitt and Paul Townsend, bassist Andy G and drummer Andy B make them a good bet on any festival bill, and Hundred Reasons remain a band to watch out for.

ILL NINO

www.illnino.com

Just as System Of A Down and Sepultura infuse their music with the rhythms and melodies of their origins (Eastern Europe and Brazil respectively), the New Jersey band Ill Nino combine their particular take on the rap-metal template with Latino influences, making for a frantic, multifaceted sound which gives them a powerful live presence. To paraphrase the famous commentator, their career has been a game of two halves.

Originally known as El Nino, the band was the project of ex-Pro-Pain drummer Dave Chavarri, whose driving force behind the considerable presence of sometime Merauder vocalist Jorge Rosado made them a live favourite in the New York area. Despite their loyal following, however, and gigs with biggies such as Fear Factory and Hatebreed, El Nino seemed destined to remain on the underground club circuit without ever achieving wider popularity.

Things changed when Chavarri's friend Max Cavalera was confronted with line-up problems in his new band, Soulfly. His drummer, Roy 'Rata' Mayorga, had

informed Cavalera of his imminent
departure, and Max was short of a
sticksman: Chavarri offered to put El Nino
temporarily on hold and stepped forward to
fill the breach for a couple of months.

The drummer returned a new man.
His time with Soulfly – one of the heaviest,
most committed bands in nu-metal – had
inspired him, and when El Nino regrouped
he attacked the live schedule with renewed
vigour. First he rechristened the band Ill
Nino (perhaps in homage to rap-rock
pioneers the Beastie Boys, whose *Licensed
To Ill* album is responsible for the careers of
half the bands in this book) and then he
revamped the entire line-up, replacing
Rosado with Brazilian-born bassist and
vocalist Christian Marchado and recruiting
Jardel Paisante (guitar), Lazaro Pina (bass)
and ex-Ricanstruction drummer Roger
Vasquez.

The new band hit the road, where it
remains to this day, having played with
bands such as Kittie, Soulfly and Snapcase.
A deal was recently struck with
Roadrunner and it seems only a matter
of time before Ill Nino takes that
all-important step upwards. Hasta la vista.

INCUBUS

www.incubusonline.com

Often falsely accused of being mere
Red Hot Chili Peppers clones,
Incubus are in fact a band which combines
funk, pop, metal, punk and even ska into its
sound with aplomb, and has managed to
build a significant following after only
two albums. Formed in 1991 in Calabasas,
California, the band consisted of singer
Brandon Boyd, guitarist Mike Einziger,
bassist Alex Katunich (later replaced by
Dirk Lance) and drummer Jose Pasillas.
After spending four years establishing a
presence on the South California
punk/metal scene, an independent album,
Fungus Amongus, was released with the aid
of the newly-recruited DJ Lyfe (Chris
Kilmore).

In 1995 the Immortal label (which was
enjoying serious sales revenue thanks to
Korn's debut album of 1994) approached
Incubus, offering a deal. The dotted line
was duly signed and a six-song taster EP of
demos, *Enjoy Incubus*, was released two years
later in preparation for a full-length album.
Laudably avoiding the urge to name their
debut record after themselves, Incubus
issued *S.C.I.E.N.C.E.* in 1998 and joined
the popular Family Values tour of the same
year. Shows with planetary acts of the
calibre of Limp Bizkit, Black Sabbath and
Korn ensued, and Incubus stayed on the
road for a gruelling two years.

But the roller-coaster of metal never
stops (bands only fall off it) and so, after a
few weeks recuperation, the band entered
the studio to record *Make Yourself*, named as
a call for individuality. It yielded a hit
single, 'Pardon Me', and another mega-tour
followed, including a jaunt with the 2000
Ozzfest.

INSANE CLOWN POSSE

www.insaneclownposse.com

Insane? Yes. Clowns? Undoubtedly. Posse? No – there's only two of them. However, the controversy that Insane Clown Posse have kicked up over their ten years as a rap-rock act has been enough for an entire battalion of clown-make-up-wearing buffoons.

Formed as an apparently serious hardcore rap outfit in Detroit in 1989, the group was originally known as Inner City Posse and consisted of several members. Planted squarely in the centre of the city's gangland territorial disputes, the band was diluted one by one until only two rappers, Violent J (Joseph Bruce) and Shaggy 2 Dope (Joseph Utsler) remained. A locally-successful single, 'Dog Beats', wasn't enough to save the group, and they folded in 1990, with J spending the following winter in jail for a variety of misdemeanours.

After a period of silence, however, the duo re-emerged from their urban hell in 1991, claiming – really – that they had received a visitation from an otherworldly troupe of circus ghosts representing something called the 'Dark Carnival'. These beings, the Posse insisted, had instructed the two Josephs to spread a warning of mankind's imminent extinction in the impending apocalypse. The message was to be spread in the form of six 'Joker Cards' (or albums). All clear? Good.

Setting up a record label, the appropriately-named Psychopathic Records, the newly-christened Insane Clown Posse released their first album *Carnival Of Carnage* in 1992, as the first so-called Joker Card. It was followed up by an EP, *Beverly Kills 50187* (50 is gang shorthand for cop, while 187 is a police radio code for homicide), but few rock fans took much notice until the release of *The Ringmaster* in 1994, a more accomplished brand of metallic hip-hop that saw the gathering of the first 'Juggalos' (dedicated ICP followers with an interest in the disturbing imagery of the Dark Carnival). Word also spread of the chaotic Posse shows, which featured fires, chainsaws and the hurling of gallons of the sickly Faygo soft drink into the audience.

All this publicity led the Jive label to sign the ICP for an album, 1995's *The Riddle Box*, which became the third Joker Card (the *Beverly Hills* record and the various other EPs which the ICP have gone on to release don't count, apparently).

INSANE CLOWN POSSE: Blame Slipknot

However, Jive's gamble didn't pay off as the album failed to sell in significant quantities: the Posse were dropped and for some time it seemed that it was all over, imminent apocalypse or not.

Their bacon was saved by the mighty Hollywood label a year later, which spent over a million dollars on the recording of Joker Card No. 4, *The Great Milenko*. In a bizarre (and very American) twist, the album was released as scheduled in July 1997, but six hours after its release Disney (Hollywood's parent company) stepped in and recalled all copies, citing obscene lyrics and 'gruesome' content. The move was widely alleged to be a conciliatory gesture to the prominent Southern Baptist protest group, which was boycotting Disney at the time for its supposedly 'anti-family' businesses (Disney subsidiary Miramax had just released *Pulp Fiction*, and Disney itself was under pressure from various slack-jawed redneck groups for the 'Gay Day' which it had introduced at Disneyland).

More fool them. The more astute Island label immediately stepped in, negotiated the rights to the ICP contract and reissued the album – which became the longest-running hip-hop album ever to remain on the *Billboard* Top 200 chart.

All was still not well, however. In 1997 Violent J was arrested for hitting a member of the crowd at an ICP gig with his microphone. Later that year, he was concussed when the Clown Posse tour bus skidded off the road. Finally, a fight at a waffle restaurant in Indiana saw both rappers go down for disorderly conduct, and J experienced an anxiety attack on stage in Minnesota – presumably in reaction to all the stress.

The band rallied in 1999, when the fifth Joker Card, *The Amazing Jeckel Brothers*, made the US Top 5. By this point, the ICP had moved into other media, producing comic books and a movie, *Big Money Hustlas*. They had also established a wrestling organisation, and made several appearances at the fights: a memorable cameo was made by Shaggy in 2000 when he fell off a steel cage and broke his nose and cheekbone.

For no immediately obvious reason, the last album to be released at the time of writing, *Bizzar* and *Bizaar* (two different versions exist) *isn't* a Joker Card – perhaps because the ICP's mission to warn mankind of his doom would then be over. In any case, the band seem to be having far too much fun getting into slanging matches with other bands, such as Coal Chamber (1999) and Slipknot (2000).

Perhaps the fact that Knot percussionist Shawn Crahan sports a clown mask made it inevitable that a clash would occur. The Posse have also moved into production, performing console duties on their labelmates Twiztid's *Mostasteless* album.

A strange story, and one that is bound to continue with many interesting twists and turns. Unless the Dark Carnival turns out to be true after all – in which case, see you in clown hell, and don't forget your red nose.

KID ROCK

www.kidrock.com

Robert James Ritchie is something of a mystery. Although his image depicts him as a white-trash refugee from the shanty towns of America (in his case, from Romeo, Michigan) he's actually a perceptive commentator on a variety of issues and is an astute operator within the music industry. To the casual observer, it might seem that he came out of nowhere in the late Nineties and rose to his current position at the top of the rap-rock pecking order in a matter of months. In fact, he's been trying to climb the greasy pole since the late Eighties, when many of today's mewling nu-metallers were still at primary school.

Born in a poor (but not destitute) household in 1971, Kid Rock spent his time listening to music (hip-hop was his main preference from its rise in the late Seventies onwards) and trying to avoid the chores that his parents – an upright, God-fearing couple – assigned to him. The family weren't averse to a spot of partying despite their religious fortitude, however, and some of Rock's earliest memories are of being summoned from his bed to a late-night gathering and being commanded to perform a cowboy dance routine – a task he would perform with great pleasure.

In fact, he later went on to become an athletic breakdancer and, once Run DMC had risen to power, there was little doubt which path his career would follow.

After doing the talent-show rounds in Detroit, the teenage Rock recorded some demos, profoundly inspired by the Beastie Boys, who were the first white kids who could rap with the best of them and not look stupid. After performing at a show hosted by Boogie Down Productions, he was approached by the Jive label, who signed him up and arranged for an album to be recorded. The result, 1990's *Grits Sandwiches For Breakfast*, was a primitive rapping effort laced with one or two riffs, but nothing to worry either the Beastie Boys or the likes of Faith No More and the Red Hot Chili Peppers. Some publicity was briefly whipped up when a local college station played the song 'Yodelin' In The Valley' (a euphemism for oral sex, it transpired) and was fined the absurd sum of $20,000 (although the penalty was later overturned on appeal), but the storm died down as quickly as it had started and Jive terminated Rock's contract.

After a move from the sticks to Brooklyn (home of the B-Boys themslves), Rock convinced the independent Continuum company to give him a deal, which led to a second album, *The Polyfuze Method*, released in 1993. Once more, his music failed to stir up much interest and the next recording, 1994's *Fire It Up* EP, appeared on his own Top Dog label. Realising that his career might be better carried forward on home turf, Rock returned to the Motor City and recorded yet another record, *Early Mornin' Stoned Pimp*, which saw the light of day (and soon after, the inside of the local record stores' bargain bins) in 1996.

Things were looking grim (Rock was even selling bootlegs of his own records to get by) but a turning point came when he decided to beef up his sound with a full rock band. Members came and went, but one permanent fixture in the line-up of what was to become Twisted Brown Trucker was Joseph Calleja (known onstage as Joe C), a dwarf who suffered from coeliac disease, which required near-constant medical attention. The other Truckers were Kenny Olson (guitar), Jason Krause (guitar), Jimmy Bones

KID ROCK: The American Bad Ass himself

(bass/keyboards), Stefanie Eulinberg (drums), backing singers Misty Love and Shirly Hayden and a DJ, Uncle Kracker (also known as Matt Shafer, an old friend of Rock's).

Suddenly everything changed: the Atlantic label signed Rock and his band and the *Devil Without A Cause* album was released in August 1998. The album risked vanishing into obscurity on its initial appearance, but Atlantic stepped up its marketing activities and, after the success of the 'Bawitdaba' and 'Cowboy' singles, Rock found himself riding a near-global wave of publicity. The album eventually went seven times platinum, helped along by the enormous success of the 'American Bad Ass' song, based on the mighty riff of Metallica's 'Sad But True'.

To capitalise on this success, Kid Rock remixed some of his older back catalogue for a compilation album, *The History Of Rock*, which helped him gain a Grammy nomination for Best New Artist (the 'New' is relative, of course), a spot at the ill-fated Woodstock 99 and the opening sequence of the 1999 MTV Music Awards. The latter was a perfect case of the wheel coming full circle – Rock jammed with Aerosmith and none other than Run DMC.

The epitaph to the Kid Rock tale is a sad one: Joe C died in his sleep in late 2000. Fans will be grateful that he lived to see his music hit the very top. As for Kid Rock himself, time will tell if the world's metal fans will require his services for very long – but then, he's used to waiting patiently in the background. Any possible dip in his fortunes is unlikely to cause him much concern.

KILKUS

www.kilkus.net

London band Kilkus were formed in May 1998 and initially comprised Paul (vocals), Chris Macaree (guitar), Chris Ransom (guitar), David Holland (bass), Chris Hayden (drums) and Ed Trowsse (DJ). Inventing the name Kilkus, which appears to be a nonsense word with no special meaning, the teenage band wrote a set's worth of heavy material influenced by Machine Head and Pantera and embarked on a tour of lowly venues – pubs, clubs and anywhere else that would have them.

The Kilkus profile grew as tours with One Minute Silence, Lostprophets and Stampin' Ground saw their playing and song writing improve, and signed to the independent Visible Noise label in early 2000. An album, *The Pattern Of Self Design*, was recorded and produced by the band themselves and released to underground acclaim, although the departure of singer Paul was an unexpected blow. However, this was resolved when Macaree moved from guitar to vocals. They are currently touring and have become a regular festival fixture.

KILL II THIS

www.angelfire.com/de/cend/kill2this.html

Another of the ever-growing new wave of British nu-metal, Kill II This have been praised in many quarters for the proficiency of their music, the power of their lyrics and the fact that they seem to be more talented than many of their more awkward, fretboard-scrubbing colleagues. The foursome have already supported Soulfly on the American/Brazilian headbangers' UK tour in 2001, and consist of Matt Pollock (vocals), Mark Mynett (guitar), Caroline Campbell (bass) and Ben Calvert (drums).

KILL II THIS: Definitely a band to watch

Campbell and Mynett first met in 1998 at the renowned Underworld club in Manchester, the band's home town. The latter had been playing in a band with the K2T name for the previous two years, and had in fact written and recorded an entire album, *Another Cross II Bear*, with the old line-up. However, he had parted ways with the other musicians just before meeting Caroline and the pair agreed to start a band under the established name. Recruiting ex-Swampdiva singer Pollock and drummer Calvert, the newly-reformed band embarked on sessions for *Deviate*, their most recent album.

The result was an underground success, and a deal is surely on its way. The publicity which Kill II This have enjoyed is almost unprecedented for an unsigned act, and it's certain that we haven't heard the last of this particular metallic bunch.

KING PRAWN

www.kingprawn.co.uk

Combining influences as disparate as punk, ska, reggae, hip-hop, jazz and metal, the music of Londoners King Prawn is a satisfyingly unpredictable blend of power and inventiveness. The band – Al-Farabi Rumjen (vocals/guitar/melodica), Devil Hands (guitar), Babar Luck (bass) and Swindonboye (drums) – formed in 1995 and spent a year rehearsing a funky, unpredictable set of tunes.

After debuting at The Garage in north London, a deal was signed with the Words Of Warning label, who had previously

worked with reggae-thrashers Dub War and punks Blaggers ITA, and a single, 'Poison In The Air', was released in January 1996. UK and overseas tours ensued and since then four albums have been released, the most recent on the Spitfire label, also home to heavyweights such as Anthrax. A fixture on both metal and hardcore scenes, the Prawns have also enjoyed plenty of press coverage and should be around for the foreseeable future.

KITTIE

http://expage.com/allkittie

A Canadian quartet formed by four schoolgirls – Morgan Lander (guitar/vocals), Fallon Bowman (guitar), Talena (bass) and Mercedes Lander (drums) – Kittie are often mocked by observers for their youth and gender before silencing those same sniggerers with the power of their music: not for nothing did Slipknot choose them as support act for their first North American tour in 1999.

Forming at high-school in 1997 and becoming known on the Canadian nu-metal scene for their live shows (which often featured Nirvana and Silverchair covers), Kittie were signed to the the Artemis label thanks to the support of Rage Against The Machine/Spineshank producer Gggarth, who had been impressed by a copy of the demo they had recorded. A full-length album, *Spit*, was released in 1999 to moderate acclaim: it appeared that the press had problems taking the band seriously despite the evident quality of their songs.

However, the message was hammered home a little harder with the following year's *Paperdoll* (Morgan: "We want to destroy the idea that a lot of men see women as blow-up dolls. We want to break that, because we're better than that"). The critical reception was more positive, perhaps thanks to the fact that Kittie were now describing themselves as 'glam-goth' or 'metal-glitter'.

Fallon Bowman left the band in early 2001 and has not been permanently replaced, though Jeff Philips has become 'touring' guitarist. Their second album *Oracle* was released in November 2001.

KITTIE: Fallon Bowman, who left the band for still-unspecified reasons in 2001.

KORN

www.korn.com

In every cultural scene, there are pioneers and there are followers. And as the saying famously goes, it's the pioneers who get all the arrows.

The undisputed leaders of nu-metal (or rap-metal, as it was known back then), from its beginnings in the early to mid-Nineties until the rise of Limp Bizkit in 1999, were undoubtedly California's finest (and weirdest) residents, Korn, originally from the town of Bakersfield, about 100 miles from Los Angeles. Few bands have simultaneously repelled the establishment and attracted fans to such a degree.

Korn revolves around the quirky, charismatic vocalist Jonathan Davis, who famously spent years working as an assistant coroner at the Kern County Coroner's Department, while also holding down a second job as an undertaker at a funeral home (he has been quoted as saying that his parents thought him strange for wanting to 'cut up dead bodies', and who can blame them?). During his career in the morgue, Davis witnessed some horrendous sights, which he occasionally incorporates into Korn's lyrics. He also addresses the theme of child abuse, from which various members of the band suffered. Other less-than-easy-listening motifs that crop up in the wonderful world of Korn are the cruelty of the schoolyard and the trials of being that American mom's nightmare, a problem child.

So where does all this angst come from, which was to fuel the lyrical musings of so many other nu-metal bands? Well, if it ain't Mom and Dad (see Kid Rock), it's the other major childhood influence – school. For years Jonathan was the sustained target of playground taunts, largely because he epitomised the anti-jock. He explains "I was into art, drama and music and I wore eyeliner" - plausible grounds for a severe kicking in the aggressively pro-sports American school environment.

Davis' daytime problems were exacerbated by the attitude of his father, a record-shop owner and music business player (he owned country singer Buck Owen's old recording studio) who "always preached... 'I'm not letting you go in the music business. You can't be in a band. You can't go and do that. You're poor one minute, you're rich the next, I don't want that kind of life for you' ". Hardly the sentiments of a sadist, one might have thought. However, the relationship clearly caused the young Jonathan some problems, although he has recently revealed that Davis Sr. is now proud of his son.

When he joined the nascent Korn in the early Nineties, Davis had recently completed a degree in Mortuary Science in San Francisco, and was fronting the local band Sexart. He was invited to join the other Korn personnel - then calling themselves LAPD (Love And Peace, Dude) - after they had seen him at a Sexart gig,

KORN: Guitarist Head – not that crucial seventh string

and the name Korn was adopted. Various apocryphal tales circulate about the origin of the name, among the most popular of which is a homosexual encounter during which a piece of sweetcorn was involuntarily expelled.

It's also rumoured that Davis was warned not to miss out on any new band that approached him during a visit to a psychic; the singer claims to have the tapes to prove it. Despite this advice, however, Davis was reluctant to leave Sexart, to whom he felt a certain degree of loyalty: however, on meeting the LAPD members, a bond rapidly developed.

steadily, ultimately going double platinum, appealing to the Generation X-ers who flocked to buy it for songs such as the uncompromising 'Ball Tongue' and Davis' lament for a destroyed childhood, the heartbreaking 'Daddy'. This sentiment was echoed on the album sleeve, a photo of a girl on a swing overshadowed by an approaching adult figure.

The band's profile grew steadily as a result of extended tours, paying off when the next album, 1996's *Life Is Peachy*, entered the US charts at No. 3 and also went double platinum. Standout tracks were the decidedly weird 'Twist' and the metallic

KORN: Singer Jonathan Davis (centre) – in full pimp rock mode

Together with the riffing of guitarists James 'Munky' Shaffer and Brian 'Head' Welch - who were among the first nu-metallers to utilise seven-string guitars - and the similarly earth-shaking bottom end of bassist Reginald 'Fieldy' Arvizu and drummer David Silveria, Korn soon developed a unique sound.

Bakersfield provided the archetypal Dullsville, USA environment for Davis and the other members, contributing to the lyrical misery of the band's 1994 debut, *Korn*, issued on Epic's Immortal imprint. Launching the career of producer Ross Robinson and arousing immediate interest among the West Coast's not-yet-nu-metal fans, the band embarked on a prolonged tour with support slots for Ozzy Osbourne, Megadeth, 311 and others. *Korn* sold

funk of 'Good God'; the latter was issued as a single with at least 15 different mixes, including live and clean versions. Korn went on to headline the 1997 Lollapalooza tour, but were forced to drop out when Munky contracted viral meningitis.

The first of many brushes with controversy occurred while Korn were recording 1998's *Follow The Leader* album (so named as a sarcastic response to the sudden wave of bands that had aped Korn's style), when a high-school student in the Michigan town of Zeeland was suspended for wearing a Korn T-shirt. The incident made the national headlines after the over-pious school principal was incautious enough to label the band's music as "indecent, vulgar and obscene" - a virtual guarantee of an extra million sales – which was helped along when Korn delivered a load of T-shirts bearing the band's name to the school.

A second whiff of scandal clings to a recent Davis tattoo - the letters HIV stand on his arm. The singer stated, "HIV is my nickname. When I first got in the band, I was so skinny they said I had AIDS, so I got it on my arm. There's some misinterpretation. Some people think it's funny, some people get pissed, I don't really care."

In true Nineties multimedia fashion, Korn began to diversify their activities after *Follow The Leader* and started working on side projects such as the weekly internet webcast Korn TV, a record label, Elementree (whose first signing was Orgy), and the mini-Lollapalooza Family Values Tour, named as a piss-take out of Dan Quayle's often-used catchphrase.

Follow The Leader was noted for the remarkable contributions of guest artists such as Limp Bizkit's Fred Durst, Ice Cube, the Pharcyde's Trevant Hardson and the blunt-puffin' Los Angeleno Cheech Marin. This time, the album reached triple platinum, helped along by the phenomenal success of the 'Got The Life' single. MTV also embraced Korn, whose 'Freak On A Leash' won in two categories at the 1999 MTV Music Video Awards. The ill-fated Woodstock 99 ("dust pits and dirt and dehydration," according to Fieldy) saw Korn play a best-of set as well as two songs from their latest album, *Issues*, released later that year.

And so Korn continue to plough their metallic furrow. The rise of Slipknot and Limp Bizkit means that their status at the top of the nu-metal tree is no longer unassailable, but they appear to be quite contented. Davis has recently become a father, and the future looks comfortable for the Bakersfield boys.

The only blot on the horizon seems to be that, having attained megastar status, some of the fans are now accusing Korn of having sold out - that age-old (and predictable) problem. The band deny this vigorously, of course, pointing out that no other group has remained as true to its principles or makes as much effort to make time for its fans as Korn. But the debate continues. It's a pivotal time for nu-metal, and the next move of Korn, who first took it to the masses, may determine whether it stands or falls.

LIBERTY 37

www.liberty37.com

One of the frontrunners in the sparse UK nu-metal scene, Liberty 37 were formed in 1997 in Swansea, Wales. Initially calling themselves Travis, Inc. the seemingly-inexorable rise of the Scottish chart-indie outfit of the same name put paid to that idea. The next name, Applecore, was received with tut-tutting by the veteran Apple label (Apple Corps – ho ho! – is one of the company's wittier Beatle-conceived trademarks), and the name Liberty 37 was settled upon in some desperation.

The band's layered, epic approach led *Kerrang!* to label their Travis, Inc. incarnation 'ones to watch' in late 1997, even drawing comparisons with the Oxford whingecore merchants Radiohead. The Org label subsequently released an L37 single, 'No Beauty', which led to a deal with the Beggars Banquet label and an EP, *Stuffed*, which appeared in May 1998.

A tour with the sadly now-defunct Bullyrag and a second single, January 1999's 'Revolution', was followed by live spots supporting Pulkas and One Minute Silence and, unhampered by some personnel difficulties, Liberty 37 recorded an album, *The Greatest Gift*. This was released after a tour with the punkish A and a spot at the Reading/Leeds festival in August.

2000 was a quieter year, but the Libertys are expected to return to the live arena soon.

LIFE OF AGONY

www.lifeofagony.com

Just qualifying for nu-metal status due to their relentless lyrical misery and crushing way with a riff, Brooklyn's pessimistically-named Life Of Agony were formed in 1989 and lasted eight years before splitting in recognition that times (and the public's musical tastes) had changed.

1993's *River Runs Red* was a powerful debut album, infused with hardcore guitar layers, but their later work swung towards a more versatile sound with a liberal dose of the melodic gloom of Nirvana – grunge was, of course, in full swing at the time. Singer Keith Caputo often performed with a hoarse but clean voice, rather like that of Nirvana vocalist Kurt Cobain, which led to several members of the press likening LOA's post-*River Runs Red* work to 'metal grunge'.

However, the power of the

as *1989-1999* and was followed by a live and rarities album, *Unplugged At Lowlands*. They remain a sorely-missed metal instution for many rockers, who found solace in Caputo's intensely personal lyrics. Oddly, his solo album, released in 2000, didn't find much favour with his erstwhile fans, who possibly found it a little lightweight compared to the work of his earlier band.

LIFE OF AGONY: Nu-metallers before the phrase was first coined

performances – which featured Caputo alternating between full-on death metal roars and the calmer, more expressive style mentioned above, assisted by guitarist Joey Z, bassist Alan Robert and ex-Type O Negative drummer Sal Abruscato – soon silenced the sceptics' cries of plagiarism, and fans gathered in significant numbers over a series of tours promoting 1995's *Ugly* and 1997's *Soul Searching Sun*. Further slots on bills featuring Ozzy Osbourne, Korn and Anthrax kept the intensely loyal fanbase happy and, despite the replacement of Abruscato with ex-Pro Pain drummer Dan Richardson, the future seemed assured.

It was a genuine shock, therefore, when Life Of Agony announced their imminent split in 1998. The move was largely due to Caputo, it seems, who felt that he would be happier pursuing other musical avenues, but many fans were distraught and were hardly consoled by the promise of a greatest hits collection. This emerged the following year

LIMP BIZKIT

www.limpbizkit.com

Although Korn were the first band to define the term 'nu-metal', Limp Bizkit are currently far and away the most well-known, by virtue of their considerable chart presence and relentless MTV exposure. The secret of their success? A nifty way with a riff, a memorable image (frontman Fred Durst's trademark red baseball cap, guitarist Wes Borland's electronic body-suit), and lashings of good old rock'n'roll cussing.

The band first came together in late 1994, when Durst, a tattooist (his arms are covered in the regulation green artwork) met bass player Sam Rivers in their home town, Jacksonville, in Florida. Rivers suggested forming a band and his cousin John Otto was recruited to play drums. Otto had trained as a jazz player but was keen to extend his skills into the rock arena. So far, so normal - until Wes Borland was brought in to play guitar. An old-school metal freak with a twisted sense of humour,

Borland's on-stage costume and antics instantly turned heads, while his adoption of black contact lenses which cover the entire cornea of both of his eyes (giving his face a weird, simian appearance) helped to spread the word.

With the initial line-up complete, all that was required was a name: Durst came up with a suitably no-brainer idea after a conversation with a friend, who had wearily told him that his brain felt like a 'limp biscuit' after a marathon dope-smoking session. Although it didn't exactly sound promising, the name appealed to the band's particular sense of frat-boy humour and the Bizkit was born.

After playing a handful of gigs in the Jacksonville area, the Limps scored a lucky break when Korn played a date in the city, riding a wave of critical praise in the wake of the release of their self-titled debut album. Korn bassist Fieldy and guitarist Head met Fred after the concert and asked

him to give them some tattoos. Striking up a friendship, the Korn musicians requested a Limp Bizkit demo and, impressed, invited Durst and his band to open for them on the next tour. More importantly, they offered to pass the tape on to Ross Robinson, who liked what he heard and offered to produce an album, as and when the band signed a record deal.

Encouraged by this development, and by the reception they received on support slots in 1995 with the Irish-American House Of Pain and Deftones, Limp Bizkit began to entertain offers from record deals. After considering the many options open to them, the band elected to sign to the small-but-cool indie label Flip, a division of Interscope.

However, in the world of nu-metal, you're nobody unless you've got a DJ in your band: the search for a suitable decksman had been going on for some time with little success. The band's tour with

LIMP BIZKIT: Frat-metal? Yob-metal? Nookie-metal? Whatever it is, the world loves it.

House Of Pain proved fortuitous: the Pain split shortly afterwards, leaving their turntablist, DJ Lethal, looking for a new outlet. The DJ was duly snapped up and the Bizkit line-up has remained unchanged ever since. "I try and bring new sounds to the band, not just the regular chirping scratching sounds," said Lethal of his role. "You won't really hear the regular, been-there-done-that scratching, know what I mean? It's all different stuff that you haven't heard before. I'm trying to be like another guitar player."

The first Bizkit long-player, *Three Dollar Bill, Y'All$*, released in July 1997 after extended local tours, was a phenomenal success: the world in general (and white America in particular) clearly felt that there was a place for a shouty, guitar-driven rap act and welcomed the Limps with open arms. The album, it must be said, was an eye-opening listen, laced with trademark Robinson production clues such as a mighty bass track, live-sounding guitar layers and drums and vocals to the fore, and had obviously benefited significantly from the considerable skills of *Nevermind* and Sepultura producer Andy Wallace, who took on mixing duties.

Songs such as 'Counterfeit' (a rant against trend-following people) and 'Pollution' (a rant against, er, loud music-hating people) were the perfect Bizkit introduction - but the album's highlight was a beefed-up version of George Michael's 'Faith' which, quite by chance, was released to coincide with the goateed smoothie's well-publicised public convenience incident.

The Limp Bizkit profile was heightened still more by the ensuing tour, which saw stage sets with a bizarre combination of science fiction-movie futurism, breakdancers and a now-legendary enormous toilet, from which the band emerged at the start of each show. A reputation started to build around the Bizkit as one of the most committed live acts around - and in fact, the band spent most of the next two years on the road. They appeared on the Warped tour of 1997, at the 1998 Ozzfest and as support acts for Faith No More and Deftones once again - all this plus a memorable spot on the original Family Values tour.

A year after Durst appeared on 'All In The Family', a track on Korn's third album, *Follow The Leader*, Limp Bizkit released

Significant Other, a monstrous album which immediately spawned a global chart hit, the very teen-friendly 'Nookie'. As the single hit the top spot in the US and Canada, the band took to the road once again, this time labelling their tour 'Ladies' Night In Cambodia' and allowing free admission to the first 200 women to turn up at every show. The ruse was a success, with girls queuing up at every concert and flocks of male fans following suit.

The album sold over 600,000 copies in its first week and would eventually sell ten times more: much of its attraction lay in the impressive roster of guests who appeared on it, including Gang Starr's DJ Premier, who produced 'N2Gether Now', a mighty rap marathon featuring the tongue-twisting skills of the Wu-Tang Clan's Method Man. Another notable cameo came from the MTV VJ Matt Pinfield, who provided a rant against anodyne pop music, while the song 'Nobody Like You' included vocals from Korn's Jonathan Davis and Stone Temple Pilot Scott Weiland. Another powerful song was 'Break Stuff', which appealed to many a jaded, resentful teenager with its call-to-arms of "If my day keeps going this way, I just might break your fuckin' face tonight..." Even Durst's mother put in a vocal performance on the album.

Wes Borland explained the title of *Significant Other* with the words: "The title refers to male-female relationships, of course. But it also refers to this record as *our* significant other. This is the record that we've wanted to make since we started this band." Durst had a different take on the album, however: "It's a record about betrayal," he said. "I guess I ask for it sometimes. The way I get treated by backstabbing friends and girls, it's probably due to my own actions."

The production crew behind *Significant Other* was another metal/grunge duo like the Robinson/Wallace team - the album was produced by Terry Date (also involved with nu-ish acts such as Pantera and White Zombie, and soon to remix Slipknot, but better-known among the cognoscenti for his Eighties work with old-school thrashers Dark Angel) and mixed by Brendan O'Brien, who had previously worked with Pearl Jam.

1998 saw the Bizkit involved in a trade scandal, in which their record label was accused of some pay-for-play payola malarkey, but both band and company

emerged unscathed and the second Family Values tour took them through to the end of the year.

And still Limp Bizkit's profile grew: Fred's public outbursts had made him a tabloid favourite along with Marilyn Manson, and the band, it seemed, might ultimately outgrow the metal scene. In nu-metal terms, 1999 belonged to Slipknot, whose self-titled debut album broke all previous records in June. Little else was happening to excite the world's legions of metal fans: Korn were sailing along in the background, seemingly content to sell a million albums here and there but not really rocking the boat, while the profusion of

FRED DURST and WES BORLAND:
The most charismatic performers in nu-metal?

new bands (of which Coal Chamber, Fear Factory, System Of A Down, Tool and Deftones were the most credible) had made the world of nu-metal a little crowded.

Oddly enough, it took the intervention of one of the giants of old metal to stir things up around Limp Bizkit. In the spring of 2000 the Metallica drummer Lars Ulrich made a series of public statements about his intention to take legal action against the software provider Napster, whose website had become an online Mecca for thousands of music fans seeking free songs. In doing so, and by throwing himself into the subsequent anti-Napster legal process with such vigour, Ulrich alienated much of Metallica's considerable fanbase - the controversy has still not died down two years later.

Limp Bizkit's response was to embark on a free tour, sponsored by Napster. Fred said: "The internet is something that's here and it's here to stay. If our fans are down with it, then we're down with it," adding that "the only people who are scared are people in the record industry... Who cares? We're going to give it to you for free, and they're going to pay for it." The reaction from fans was loud and overwhelmingly positive, while the genius behind the move from both companies was evident: the Bizkit were perceived as rebels against the establishment, represented by Metallica (who had in any case been criticised by many fans since the early Nineties for their move away from thrash metal to chart-friendly rock), while Napster were seen to be allying themselves with the hottest new band on the block. Marketing experts worldwide shook their heads in mute admiration.

He finished his tirade with the words, "I'll be your scapegoat". At another show, Fred was arrested and accused of kicking a security guard in the head, after the singer reacted to the way in which the guard handled a stage-invading fan at a gig in Minnesota. Durst announced from the stage: "I kicked that punk-ass security guard in the head. That fuckin' bitch, you ain't gonna get a cheque tonight!" The case was later settled out of court, bringing a busy year (for the lawyers as well as the band) to a close.

One more step remained before Limp Bizkit could achieve truly planetary status, and this was taken when it was revealed that they would rework the theme tune to

LIMP BIZKIT: For better or Durst, the biggest nu-metallers of them all

1999 still had more Bizkit-related controversy to come, however: Woodstock 99, held in June, saw fans riot during the band's performance of 'Break Stuff'. The aggression peaked with the alleged rape of a 24-year-old woman. Later in the year, Durst told the *Dotmusic* website that "Promoters and people who were greedy did some things wrong... Different personalities, different people and lots of drugs formed the ingredients for a disaster. We looked out in front of us and there's 100,000 people going off, looking like they're having a blast. The next thing you know, [people are saying] 'You guys ruined Woodstock!'."

Mission: Impossible 2, the effects-heavy blockbuster starring Tom Cruise. At first sight this wasn't a particularly engaging idea: the first *Mission* film, released in 1997, had featured a rather dull take on the famous theme, recorded by Adam Clayton and Larry Mullen Jr. of U2. However, the Bizkit's version was astounding: Borland and Otto had created a tense, slow-building soundscape based on the song's distinctive opening triads, before bursting into a fully metallic chorus. It was Durst's angst-ridden lyrics, however - "I know why you wanna hate me!" - which laid out the Bizkit manifesto and sold the song to the world.

The song, renamed 'Take A Look Around', won Best Rock Video at the 2000 MTV Video Awards and preceded two other singles, 'My Generation' and 'Rollin'' - the latter the heaviest work that the band have ever produced, with Durst's vocal more guttural than his trademark mid-range whine, and ironic references to "the moshpit" and "old-school metal soldiers". 'Rollin'' also boasted a $3 million video, with Fred cruising pimp-style in a Rolls-Royce cabriolet.

In October, Limp Bizkit released the somewhat offputtingly-titled third album, *Chocolate Starfish And The Hot Dog Flavored Water* (Fred: "People are always calling me an asshole - so I thought I'd make it the title of the album"). The record went straight to No. 1 in several countries and sold over a million copies in a week - the first rock album ever to do so. Refreshingly, the album contained more mellow moments than previous long-players, with Borland's treated guitar sounds often a chilled-out marvel and Durst sometimes sounding rather contented. Borland commented: "It's a third level as a combination of *Significant Other* and the heaviness of *Three Dollar Bill, Y'all$*, but more mature, and focused in a better way".

Celebrities to appear in the world of Limp Bizkit at this point included Eminem and Christian Aguilera: in his single at the time, 'The Real Slim Shady', the former alleged that Aguilera had provided a certain sexual favour for Fred, who told MTV: "It's not true, so it doesn't bother me. I think she's an amazing singer. She's gonna have longevity. I like her and I've talked to her a couple of times and that's that." For anyone who had failed to get the message, Fred helpfully added: "She's never sucked my dick." Eminem himself — who had appeared in the 'Break Stuff' video — must have found all the uproar amusing.

Christina and Fred went on to perform a duet at the MTV Video Music Awards, to many Bizkit fans' surprise: but when asked to explain himself in an interview held at the Playboy Mansion, Durst paraphrased his own lyrics by explaining "I already told you guys before - I did it all for the nookie, man. That's why I did that with Christina. I want that girl, that's that." Warming to his theme, he elaborated: "What do you want? I don't want to make *music* like her. I can't stand that kind of music. People were like, 'What'd you do that for?' What do you *think* I did that for? It's obvious, isn't it? You know what I mean."

Durst's ability to get along with other musicians has not always been so evident, however. One memorable occasion saw him suffer an unexplained fit of pique while performing at the Krock Dysfunctional Family Picnic concert, shouting "I want to dedicate this next song to the lead singer of Creed - that guy is an egomaniac. He's a fucking punk and he's backstage right now acting like fucking Michael Jackson." To make his point quite clear, he observed: "Fuck that motherfucker and fuck you too!" Durst later told MTV that after the show, Creed gave him an anger management manual signed by the band.

Other gigs have seen more serious occurrences. In January 2001, at the Big Day Out three-day festival in Sydney, a girl in the audience crush died of a heart attack during Limp Bizkit's set: the band pulled out the following day. Organisers blamed "excessive heat and crowd excitement" rather than the band themselves, but the Bizkit stated that the tragedy could have been avoided. "We basically begged the promoter to increase security measures and were told that he has been doing the event for 10 years, and that he knows what he's doing, and to leave him alone," said Fred.

In true Noughties style, Fred has spread his activities over a wide variety of arenas: he was famously made a vice-president of Interscope and signed the band Staind, while he also produced the second album from his fellow Jacksonville rap-metallers Cold. Furthermore, he personally directed the videos for 'Faith', 'Nookie' and 'My Way', and has guested on albums by Videodrone and Soulfly as well as the earlier Korn cameo. Rumours have even circulated that he is writing a screenplay for a film - the mind boggles. But Fred doesn't care - "Look at George Lucas!" he told one interviewer. "That motherfucker, he don't stop, dude! If we do enough amazing things - films, videos, songs, music - you become legends, and a whole new generation becomes tripped-out to work with you." He's putting his money where his mouth is by working on a movie, saying that the film, *Runts*, will explore teenage violence and alienation in America. He told MTV: "Crazy things are happening that don't need to be happening, and people are retaliating in the wrong way. This movie needs to happen now."

There's a lot of life yet, it seems, in the self-confessed "redneck fucker from Jacksonville" and his band. Limp Bizkit have promised that the next album will be the "heaviest album you've ever heard". Durst said, "We're gonna go in, no air-conditioning, 130 degree room, just mad as fuck. We have a lot to say now and we're really emotional."

His promise of "the heaviest album you've ever heard" doesn't wash with those familiar with the extreme metal approach of Deicide, Nile and Slayer, but most of the Bizkit's fans aren't. Only a seismic shift in popular music itself will, it seems, be enough to unseat the Bizkit from their current position on the throne of nu-metal, despite the shock departure of Borland in the autumn of 2001. For now, they reign supreme, and if Durst's talent matches his ambition (and the size of his mouth), they'll be around for some time to come.

LINEA 77: Powerful Italian nu-metal

LINEA 77

www.linea77.com

An Italian nu-metal band formed in 1993 in Turin, Linea 77 first came to the public's attention after their first demo, *Ogni Cosa Al Suo Posto* (which translates as Everything In Its Place), appeared the following year. The local Dracma label released a second recording, *Kung Fu*, and the band spent time touring in Italy. A Milanese label, Black And White, offered Linea 77 a contract after the success of the second tape and released a full-length album, *Too Much Happiness Makes Kids Paranoid*.

It was a move to the seminal Earache label in Nottingham which made the band a truly international force, however, and the 23-date tour which the label organised for them. An Earache album, *Ketchup Suicide*, was being recorded at the time of writing.

LINKIN PARK

www.linkinpark.com

Still trying to shake off an undeserved 'metal boy-band' tag applied by snide journalists out for a cheap laugh, the youthful five-piece Linkin Park were formed in the late Nineties in southern California. Originally titled Hybrid Theory, the genesis of the band occurred at high school when rapper Mike Shinoda, guitarist Brad Delson and drummer Rob Bourdon struck up a teenage friendship. After graduation, Mike met up with fellow student and DJ Joseph Hahn at a local college, the Pasadena Art Center.

The move that made them stand out from the legions of big-shorted teen-metallers, however, was the recruitment of another singer, the Arizona-born Chester Bennington, who provided a deep roar as a complement to Hahn's mid-range rapping. The rechristened band began to play gigs, notably at LA's famous Whisky A-Go-Go – where they were famously offered a publishing deal after their very first show.

Showcase gigs followed and, as the nu-metal virus spread and half-decent rap-rock bands became the LA A&R man's primary target, a deal was ultimately signed with Warners. The debut album, *Hybrid Theory* (that name was always going to come in useful), was released in late 2000 and, thanks to the enormous international success of the 'Crawling' single, was still selling by the wagonload at the time of writing. A textured, atmospheric record, the band's self-declared Deftones, Aphex Twin and Nine Inch Nails influences made it a dark, mesmerising listen.

Thanks to their way with a sneering rap and their MTV-friendly good looks, Linkin Park have won the support of thousands of teenage metal fans in a matter of months - but they still have to endure the odd Boyzone comparison. Mind you, producing a multi-platinum album has to make the taunts easier to bear, eh, chaps?

LINKIN PARK: Rapper Mike Shinoda and his band represent the commercial side of nu-metal more than any other outfit.

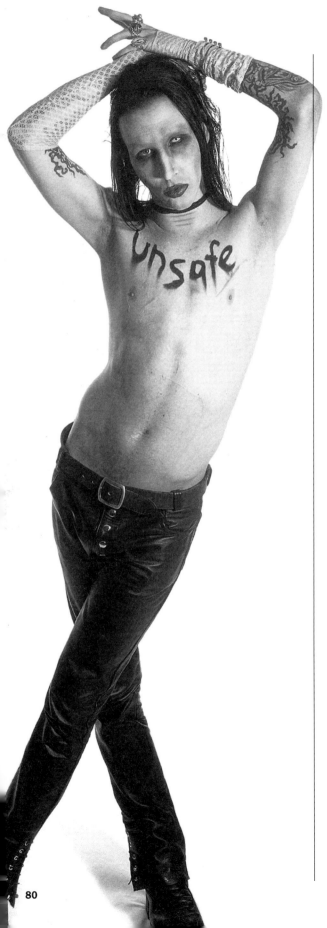

MARILYN MANSON

www.marilynmanson.net

Few bands can claim to have upset as many members of the establishment as Marilyn Manson, also the stage name of its lead singer, a skinny teen icon formerly known as Brian Warner and prone to delivering outstanding soundbites. The cause of all the outrage stems largely from the fact that the world's kids love Brian and his band's freakishly catchy tunes with a genuinely disturbing vigour, rather than because the group itself does anything particularly disgusting. The message that Manson broadcasts in lyrics, visual image and interviews is anti-Christian, anti-social and unorthodox, it's true, but the band are hardly the Sex Pistols or Anal Cunt, displaying a musical and lyrical sophistication lacking in many other bands of this ilk.

Wandering from standard metal to glam rock to electronica-tinged industrial sounds and back, Marilyn Manson can also hardly be labelled merely a nu-metal band – although their early albums were a far cry from the versatility they display today. Since their formation in Florida way back in 1989 (eons ago in nu-metal terms), the band has recruited and shed members at a prodigious rate, improving its musical and composing skills at the same time. The original line-up revolved around Manson (vocals) but also featured Daisy Berkowitz (guitar), Olivia Newton-Bundy (bass), Zsa Zsa Speck (keyboards) and Sara Lee Lucas (drums). The concept – which should reveal much about the topical obsessions of the group's leader – was that each player would adopt the first name of a female icon and the surname of a serial killer. No wonder the parents got scared.

Bundy and Speck gave way to the charmingly-named Madonna Wayne Gacy and Gidget Gein, before the band was signed by Nine Inch Nails' Trent Reznor to his new label, Nothing. The first Marilyn Manson album, 1994's *Portrait Of An American Family* (released after the replacement of Gein with Twiggy Ramirez) caused little concern for most people, however – fans, critics or otherwise.

A scratchy, primitive metal record, it sold relatively few copies, although tours with perve-metallers Genitorturers and hardcore punks Suicidal Tendencies (now *there's* an odd pairing if I ever saw one) raised the MM profile significantly in their home state. *Portrait's* main claim to fame was that it was partially mixed at the house where the infamous Sharon Tate murders had taken place at the hands of Charles Manson and his followers.

Later work, such as 1996's *Mechanical Animals*, saw a much greater level of sophistication, however: a direct homage to the pansticked days of glam rock, it disseminated the Manson message to a much wider audience. Lucas had been replaced by Ginger Fish by this point, while the guitarist Zim Zum had also joined the ranks.

In 1998 Manson announced that *Mechanical Animals* had been the first of an intended concept trilogy, and the second of the three, *Antichrist Superstar*, became even more popular than its predecessor. Based on the idea of an anti-superhero in the form of Warner, the band professed surprise when fans took it literally and began to regard their idol as some kind of messiah. A suitabley sarcastic single, 'The Beautiful People', went on to be Manson's wake-up call for the majority of the American populace, reaching No. 3 on the *Billboard* listings. A cover of the Eurythmics' 'Sweet Dreams' also sold well, allowing mainstream radio to play Manson's music without fear of censorship from the many right-wing groups which had begun to bluster at the band's rise to public prominence.

In 2000, the third chapter, *Holy Wood (In The Shadow of the Valley of Death),* was released, featuring a crucified Manson – lacking his lower jaw – as its cover art. It sold hugely, delighting fans with its scope, which included 'The Fight Song' (later to be remixed by Slipknot's Joey Jordison). By this stage Marilyn himself had become a priest in the Church of Satan and, along with Limp Bizkit's Fred Durst, was more or less the most feared tabloid figure in America – by the rednecks, at least: the kids love him.

And so the freakshow goes on. Granted, you may not enjoy the sight of the Reverend Manson dressed on-stage as the Pope, or – as he inexplicably tends to do –

exposing his buttocks to the crowd. But you've got to give him credit. He knows his act is just that – an act. And as such, he may well have the last laugh.

MARILYN MANSON: You're not going out looking like that, young man

MERAUDER

One of the great unsung New York metalcore heroes of the Nineties (for some reason, mainstream recognition all seemed to go to the equally influential Biohazard), Merauder earned a degree of recognition as far back as 1990 for their insanely powerful shows supporting Morbid Angel, Carnivore, Sick Of It All and Motörhead.

Two 1992 demos and a split 7" single with their fellow New Yorkers Stigmata led to a deal three years later with Century Media, who had also been impressed with the band's contribution to the seminal *East Coast Assault* compilation. An album was recorded and produced by Cro-Mags guitarist Parris Mayhew and entitled *Master Killer*; its underground success led to a tour with Fear Factory. The line-up consisted at this point of vocalist Jorge, guitarist Sob, ex-Candiria bassist Mike and sometime Leeway and Both Worlds drummer Pokey.

A second album was named after the classic martial arts movie *Five Deadly Venoms* and produced by Both Worlds member A.J. Novello in late 1998 and early 1999. It too sold well, but the band's future was put in jeopardy by Jorge's departure to Ill Nino.

MERCURY RAIN: Technical, progressive and satisfyingly heavy

MERCURY RAIN

www.mercuryrain.com

One of the more promising acts on the current independent metal scene is Bristol's Mercury Rain, based around the formidable songwriting and performing talents of noted producer Jon Hoare. Having honed his vision in the speed metal bands Undertaker and Crisis in the late Eighties and early Nineties, Hoare realised that the metal-buying public's tastes had become more versatile and in 1998 set about forming a power metal band with Gothic and electronic elements.

The result was an eclectic grouping of accomplished musicians, whose line-up fluctuated for some time before stabilising as Sonia Porzier (ex-Tears Of Ea, vocals), Hoare (bass) and Andy Pester (drums). Various guitarists have come and gone. Each member brought a distinctive set of influences to the group, from the old-school thrash sound of Running Wild to more recent rap-metal acts such as Just Like Her.

A sought-after limited-edition EP, *Where Angels Fear*, was subsequently recorded and self-released, and was acclaimed in the international media for its deft blend of expertly-layered atmospherics and uncompromising riffing. The band continue to tour, and a major deal is now surely only a matter of time.

METHODS OF MAYHEM

www.methodsofmayhem.com

Sick of the endless internecine bickering within his legendary rock band Mötley Crüe, drummer Tommy Lee formed a rap-metal band with industrial touches in 1998. Lee had come to feel that his main band, a fixture in the rock world since the mid-Eighties, had become somewhat old-fashioned in the wake of grunge and hip-hop, despite their occasional attempts to update their image. Although he had formed MoM before actually leaving Crüe, he realised – correctly – that fans wouldn't take him seriously if he didn't commit to the project full-time and decided to quit while he was ahead, bidding farewell to his big-haired bandmates some months later.

In September 1999 Methods Of Mayhem signed to MCA and an album was scheduled for release. Word spread rapidly: Mötley and rap-metal fans were keen to hear the fruits of Tommy's vision, especially once it was revealed that a host of stars had turned out to make guest appearances on the record. As it turned out, the self-titled album boasted cameos by Kid Rock, George Clinton, Mixmaster Mike of the Beastie Boys, Scott and Ken of the Crystal Method, Limp Bizkit's Fred Durst, U-God of the Wu-Tang Clan, Snoop Dogg and Lil' Kim, making it a multifaceted record, if also one without much of an individual identity.

Fans snapped it up, pleased with Lee's competent performance on guitar, bass, drums and vocals and that of his co-composer Tim Murray, who went by his stage name of Tilo. A memorable video, starring Durst, Clinton and Lil' Kim, accompanied the single 'Get Naked' (possibly inspired by Lee's infamous home video of himself and his then-wife Pamela Anderson) and the band seemed to be established in the fans' affections. A second album is due to appear, although whether Lee will choose to make Methods Of Mayhem a long-term project is as yet unknown.

METHODS OF MAYHEM: Ex-Mötley Crüe drummer Tommy Lee

MINDSET

From Virginia Beach, Mindset were formed in 1994 by guitarist Don Campbell and bassist John O'Neil, who completed the line-up with singer Roddy Lane and drummer Kenny Windley. The band's early sound was compared to Tool and Korn (the latter's funk-laden grooves and downtuned riffing were inescapable at the time) although later work harked back to earlier influences such as Deep Purple.

After the release of a four-track EP,

a deal was signed with the Noise label and a self-titled album appeared in late 1997. Production was handled by fader-twiddlers Brad Divens (who had produced Souls At Zero) and Drew Mazurek (who had worked with Texas Is The Reason). A possibly anti-sports metal single, 'The Devil Wore Adidas', became a radio hit around the same time.

Campbell was replaced by Johnny Smallwood at around the time of the album's release, but the band soldiered on nonetheless, producing another album, *A Bullet For Cinderella*, in 1998, again with Divens and Mazurek. A high point of the album was a brief cameo by Nothingface singer Matt Holt on 'Die, Ricki Die'. Tours of Europe and the US followed in 1999.

MINUS 313

www.minus313.com

An act that combines metal, punk and a host of other influences to become what they believe is a broader concept than mere 'nu-metal', the US East Coast's Minus 313 was formed in 1997 and produced a demo, the hardcore-indebted *In The Wrong*. The band – Justin James (vocals), Scott Harrington (guitar), Ray Michaud (guitar, keyboard), Dumas (bass) and Justin Mothersele (drums) – immediately embarked on intensive touring in the area, playing with bands such as Biohazard, Static-X and Puya and also scoring a spot on the US Ozzfest.

Signing to the Burning Kind label in 1999, Minus 313 issued an album, *By Any Means Necessary*, and a single, 'First Stone Cast', which demonstrated their powerful, almost psychedelic sound, influenced by Ultraspank, Mindfunk, Blind Melon, Helmet and Prong. The tunes themselves were explained by the band as "an intensely cathartic release of our pent-up frustration... In a lot of ways it's both hope and disappointment rolled up into an emotional breakdown set to slamming rhythms."

The Minus profile was consolidated in 2000 by a second album, *Carefactor: Zero*, which was supported once more by extended touring. The band's work appeared on several compilations, including the *East Coast Assault* set issued by the seminal Too Damn Hype label. They remain an underground band to watch.

MIOCENE

www.mioceneonline.co.uk

Perhaps the closest thing that Britain's nu-metal scene has to the art-rock experimentation of Tool, East London's Miocene perform dark, thoughtful music with plenty of power but a long way removed from the simple riffing of less talented bands. Formed in 1999 and consisting originally of three school friends, singer Ben, guitarist Graham and bass player Alex, the band would spend a lot of quality time jamming together at their friend Lee's house, with a certain amount of 'herbal' support.

MIOCENE: Hard-hitting but experienced

Drummer Leo was recruited after the volume of his playing awoke Ben, who was hungover after a sociable night out. Previously an aficionado of various East End hardcore clubs, Leo had maintained a straightedge lifestyle until joining Miocene, but this didn't last long. The new four-piece found themselves in demand on the UK's metal scene, building a definite buzz before even recording a demo. Shows with Lostprophets, Hundred Reasons and Medulla Nocte led to a demand for recorded material, and a self-produced sampler gained independent radio airplay despite the fact that mastering had not yet been completed.

The Infernal label released an EP, *Refining The Theory*, in late 2000, which received plenty of positive press, and led to a step up supporting established names such as Crazytown, Mudvayne, Clutch and Sunna. Sessions for a full-length album were underway as this book went to press, and given the band's eclectic tastes and willingness to experiment (Massive Attack are a known Miocene favourite) the result should be well worth the wait.

MISERY LOVES CO.

www.miserylovesco.com

A much-missed pioneering industrial metal act, the Swedish Misery Loves Co. was formed in 1993 by Patrik Wiren (vocals) and Orjan Ornkloo (guitar, bass, keyboards). The former had previously played with Midas Touch (signed at one point to the German Noise label), while the latter had played with several unsigned Swedish acts.

Specialising from the start in dark, electronic soundscapes and singing about sex and death in an almost gothic vein, MLC's first recorded effort was 'Sonic Attack', produced for the *Extreme Close Up* compilation. This led to a deal with the MNW Zone label, which had previously worked with Clawfinger – a band with which Misery would have a long association.

The first album, a self-titled recording, was released in 1995. Nottingham's Earache label (known for keeping an ear to the ground for new European acts) signed the band and re-released the album in various European territories, which the band supported with tours. The live band consisted of Wiren and Ornkloo plus Jim Edwards (guitar), Marre Ericksson (bass)

MISERY LOVES CO.: Soon to resurface

and Olle Dahlstedt (drums – although he would be replaced and return several times in the band's career).

Shows with Clawfinger, Warrior Soul and Headskin in Europe followed, before the album was reissued in the States, with bonus remixes from Killing Joke and Pitchshifter. A 7-track EP, *Happy*, pushed the band to the next level, and concerts in 1997 with Fear Factory and Slayer brought MLC to a far wider audience. A still wider fanbase developed when the second album, *Not Like Them* (1997) reached No. 12 on *Kerrang!*'s Top 20 Albums of the year, an achievement endorsed by crowds who witnessed their support slot with Machine Head.

Misery's finest hour is generally thought to be their third and final album, *Your Vision Was Never Mine To Share*, released in March 2000. The power element had been ratcheted up, along with the bevy of dark, threatening samples: the public were keen, but before a European tour with Kill II This and Earthtone 9 could be completed, the band mysteriously announced their split. This sudden change of fortunes was never fully explained and many fans were left somewhat confused, as MLC were perceived to be at the peak of their powers.

And so the Misery story ends – although the players themselves may resurface in the future. Such is life, eh?

MONDO GENERATOR

The sporadically-active side project of Queens Of The Stone Age bassist Nick Oliveri, Mondo Generator consists of QOTSA guitarist Josh Homme, drummers Brant Bjork and Up N. Syder (ahem) as well as the generously-bearded Oliveri himself, under the nom de guerre of Rex Everything.

Known as he is for his fondness for 'nose products' (as he put it to Q magazine in 2000), the fact that Oliveri's first (and to date, only) MG album is titled *Cocaine Rodeo* comes as little surprise to those in the know. An album of suitably quirky rock, it is notable for its cover art, a shot of the manically-grinning four-stringer delving into a party-sized stack of beer and coke. Amusingly meaningless.

MR BUNGLE

www.bunglefever.com

Before singer Mike Patton ever turned heads with the strange sounds of Faith No More and Fantomas, he had honed his unusual songwriting approach in his high-school band Mr. Bungle, named after a character in an educational film who was supposed to warn schoolchildren off various nefarious activities.

The band - Patton, guitarist Trey Spruance, bassist Trevor Dunn, tenor saxophonist/clarinettist Clinton McKinnon, alto saxophonist Theo Lengyel and drummer Danny Heifetz - formed in 1985 in their home-town of Eureka in California and immediately startled gig-goers with their aggressive, unhinged approach. Patton and Spruance adopted the names Vlad Dracula and Scummy and the whole band wore masks on stage (is this ringing any bells, Slipknot fans?).

A series of demos were recorded, with titles such as *The Raging Wrath Of The Easter Bunny*, *Bowl Of Chiley*, *Goddammit I Love America* and *OU818*. One of these primitive but fascinating recordings came to the attention of the rap-metal collective Faith No More, whose singer Chuck Mosely had left the band and who were searching for the right person to fill the vocals spot.

FNM duly offered Patton the job, but he decided to continue singing with both bands rather than splitting his earlier outfit up: the enormous success of Faith No More's *The Real Thing* album allowed him to mention his other band repeatedly in interviews, and perhaps on the strength of this, Warners made Mr Bungle an offer.

Enlisting the fearsomely experimental producer John Zorn to work on the self-titled debut album, Warners saw their newest signing rise to cult popularity in a matter of months, helped along by bizarre live shows featuring covers such as the *Star Wars* theme. However, Patton's involvement in Faith No More - whose 1991 set *Angel Dust* saw them fly still higher (no pun intended) - meant that he couldn't devote much time to the project and the other members formed other bands: Spruance with Faxed Head, Dieselhed and Zip Code Rapists, and Spruance, Dunn, and Heifetz with the Secret Chiefs 3.

When Jim Martin left Faith No More, Spruance replaced him for a time, recording guitar parts for the less-successful *King For A Day... Fool For A Lifetime* album, but that was the extent of his work with Patton's day-job band and the next real Bungle product was 1995's *Disco Volante*. A world tour followed, but once more the band were hampered by Patton's other commitments and four years passed (during which FNM split) before another album appeared. 1999's *California* did moderately well once again, but by this time it was apparent that Patton's interests lay elsewhere, specifically with his Fantomas project and his newly-launched Ipecac label. Still, it was fun while it lasted, and for all we know Mr Bungle may well reappear some day in appropriately bizarre form.

MUDDER

www.thirtyfiveinchmudder.com

Before the spectacular rise of Slipknot in 1999, the name of Des Moines, Iowa's capital city, meant almost nothing to the world's music fans. The archetypal Dullsville, USA (see the Knot's own entry for a comprehensive explanation), Des Moines has developed a thriving metal scene in the wake of its most famous sons' rise to infamy, which has been spearheaded by a band called Mudder, although ex-Slipknot singer Anders Colsefni's band Painface has also played an important role in this.

Formed in 1996, for the next four years the band went by the name 35 Inch Mudder, but dropped the first half on realising that too many metal bands were using numbers in their names (Powerman 5000 and Linea 77 are just two such that appear in these pages). The parallels between Mudder (whose line-up consists of singers Dust and C-Bone, guitarist Camel, bassist Chad and drummer Dan) and Slipknot are more apparent than merely their shared city of origin: for example, both acts spent the first few years of their career slogging away on the local Iowan club and festival circuit, building up fanbases in the relatively close cities of Omaha and Chicago. Furthermore, both bands produced their first work at SR Audio, a studio situated in the Des Moines suburb of Urbandale, and worked with a local producer called Sean McMahon. Finally, both outfits have toured almost incessantly with a variety of acts: in Mudder's case, supporting bands as diverse as Megadeth, Machine Head, Anthrax, Fear Factory, Motley Crue, Papa Roach, Taproot, Staind and Limp Bizkit.

All this hard work has not been without its rewards: the McMahon-produced EP *Stained* has sold over 6,000 copies, and a full-length album is scheduled for release. Good luck to them, and if they do as well as their psychotic masked fellow Iowans, the Midwest is in for a noisy few years.

MUDVAYNE

www.mudvayne.com

Like Orgy and Coal Chamber, Mudvayne burst into most metal fans' awareness with an apparently fully-formed and polished image, message and style of their own. The quartet wear intricately-detailed make-up, wax lyrical about futuristic subjects and look simultaneously grim and laughable.

The truth, of course, is that they spent years honing their act. Formed in the less-than-metallic environs of Peoria, Illinois, in 1996, the line-up eventually settled as Kud (vocals), Gurrg (guitar), Ryknow (bass) and Spag (drums). Like Mudvayne, the initial parallels with fellow small-towners Slipknot are immediately apparent: both bands self-released a debut album – in the case of Mudvayne, the oddly-titled *Kill I Oughta* – and both released an almost spitefully heavy album after signing a record deal, which they later referred to as their 'first' record. Both acts also used a name producer to channel their bile into recorded form. In the 'Vayne's case this album was *LD 50*, issued in August 2000 after a deal was inked with Epic, and the producer was Garth Richardson (Rage Against The Machine, L7, Spineshank), who usually signs his name 'Gggarth' as an ironic nod to his stutter.

The album reflects Mudvayne's interest in both classic science fiction and psychology. The record's first track is 'Monolith' – after the mysterious black artefact that appears throughout Stanley Kubrick's classic *2001: A Space Odyssey* – while the album title itself is a medical term used by chemists to denote a substance that is toxic enough to kill fifty out of any hundred humans that take it. Britney Spears this ain't.

MUDVAYNE: Just imagine the laundry bills

Knot comparisons became truth when the Iowan nine-piece took Mudvayne on the road in 2000. Their clown-masked percussionist Shawn Crahan also took on executive production duties on *LD 50*. Finally, both bands appeared on 2000's Tattoo The Earth bill, becoming firm friends along the way. Mudvayne have reacted with annoyance when journalists have compared them to Slipknot, however – the constant references must have taken their toll. Just don't use the words 'Knot' and 'protegés' in the same sentence.

long-player, 1998's *The Weapon*, which was followed up by a mighty 55-date European tour with Biohazard, but trouble was brewing despite the rapturous reception they received. First the band parted ways with their label, Century Media, and then a new singer, David 'Sailor' Bryant, and a new drummer, Danny Murphy, were recruited.

The change of line-up and label appeared to breathe fresh life into the band, which achieved its best reviews yet for 2000's self-released *Deadly*.

MY OWN VICTIM

www.myownvictim.com

A hardcore metal band not from the mean streets of Brooklyn or Chicago but from the comparatively placid environs of Louisville in Kentucky, My Own Victim formed in 1994 and recorded an album, *Burning Inside*, the following year, for a local indie label. For some reason it was Europe rather than America that took the band to its bosom, and the band built a devoted festival following thanks to appearances on the German and Dutch summer shows.

The band, Vic Hillerich (vocals), Jeff Toy and Brian Omer (guitars), Todd Conn (bass) and a drummer friend, took steps forward with their second

MY RUIN

www.myruin.com

A relatively new band centring on the impassioned vocals of singer Tairrie B, My Ruin formed when Tairrie left her old group, Tura Satana, which had been a minor success on the goth/glam metal scene, issuing a couple of albums in the mid-Nineties.

The first My Ruin recording, an album called *Speak And Destroy*, was more or less a solo project backed up by a touring band and failed to gain much attention. However, after Tairrie assembled a much more meaningful set of musicians (ex-Movement guitarist Mick Murphy, bassist Meghan Mattox, and Downset

drummer Chris Hamilton for the studio – live drums are handled by ex-Tung stickswoman Yael), the resulting long-player, *A Prayer Under Pressure Of Violent Anguish*, was a far more rounded recording and attracted serious critical acclaim.

The album contained covers of Nick Cave's 'Do You Love Me?' and Black Flag's 'My War', and reflected Tairrie's obsessions with Catholicism and sexuality, couched in a deeply emotional set of songs, with her vocal a guttural, shredded scream. My Ruin's self-avowed mission to combat the anodyne Limp Bizkits of the world is helped along by Tairrie's propensity for controversial soundbites, and the band looks set for a measure of success, especially as it is one of the few female-led nu-metal acts.

MY RUIN: Singer Tairrie B in reflective mood

NAILBOMB

A collaboration between now-Soulfly/then-Sepultura frontman Max Cavalera and Fudge Tunnel guitarist Alex Newport, Nailbomb was a chance for the Brazilian guitarist and activist to show his more punkish side and combine it with certain electronic elements, provided courtesy of Newport and Fear Factory guitarist Dino Cazares, who also guested.

The first album, a self-titled recording featuring the talents of Sepultura members Igor Cavalera (drums) and Andreas Kisser (guitar) as well as six-stringer Ritchie Bujnowski of Wicked Death, was an

festival in 1995 and featured a Jello Biafra song and a guest appearance on bass guitar by Evan Seinfeld of Biohazard. As a consolation for fans who mourned their heroes' passing, Cavalera's sleevenotes explained that the band had never been designed to be a long-term project: "Nailbomb was always meant to be short, to the point, and fun."

NERVE ENGINE

www.nervengine.com

On the brink of a deal at the time of writing, Barnsley's Nerve Engine have built an international following thanks largely to their intelligent use of the internet as a marketing tool, topping download charts on several alternative music sites and continuing to expand their national following through constant touring.

NAILBOMB: Max Cavalera is second from right

appropriately driven project, attacking the establishment in true punk style in a rawer, more unfocused way than the political diatribes of Sepultura. Welcomed by punk-metal fans worldwide, the record became a fixture in underground rock clubs.

The bandmembers knew that Nailbomb was merely a side project, however, and a second album, the live *Proud To Commit Commercial Suicide*, was the last word on the subject of Nailbomb. Eleven of the 13 tracks were recorded at Holland's Dynamo

Guitarist David Diley first assembled the band in 1998, recruiting singer Kris Allen, fellow six-stringer Mark Burrows, bass player Gary Solomon and drummer Andrew Richards and recording a demo the following summer. A second recording, *Seven Days*, was distributed on the web in mid-2000 and became a featured download on many mainstream sites. An album was slated for release in 2001, making Nerve Engine one of the few metal bands at the forefront of the nascent web-based music industry to have made much impact.

NICKELBACK

www.nickelback.com

A Canadian band recently taken under the wing of Roadrunner and making a name for itself in spite of the mighty noise being made by the label's bigger acts such as Slipknot and Fear Factory, Nickelback was named after bassist Mike Kroeger (who worked at a branch of the Starbucks coffee chain in Vancouver) handed a customer five cents' change for a $1.45 purchase for the several thousandth time.

The band was formed in 1996 by Kroeger and his vocalist brother Chad, who recruited their cousin Brandon, a drummer, and a guitarist friend, Ryan Peake. After releasing a seven-track demo, *Hesher* (a slurred version of the phrase, 'Hey, sure'), and a self-financed album, *Curb*, a local buzz was in place, despite the fact that Brandon was the first of no fewer than six drummers. The most recent arrival is Ryan Vikedal.

NICKLEBACK: Rock songs, but the lyrical misery of grunge

A second album was recorded, mixed by Garth Richardson. *The State* was released in January 1999 and was a Canadian hit, with the single 'Leader Of Men' a chart entry. After Roadrunner became involved, Nickelback embarked on tour with a wide variety of bands, including Stabbing Westward, Creed and Silverchair.

At the time of writing, Nickelback is preparing for the release of *Silver Side Up*, a powerful new collection which addresses issues such as domestic abuse. They remain one of the few Canadian acts to make much impact on the nu-metal scene – which is unusual, as the echelons of Eighties and Nineties extreme metal featured dozens of accomplished Canadian bands.

NINE INCH NAILS

www.nin.com

Along with Ross Robinson, Max Cavalera, Fred Durst, Dino Cazares and Jonathan Davis, Nine Inch Nails' Trent Reznor is one of the most influential ringmasters in the mad circus of nu-metal. His name is inextricably linked to industrial rock, a bleak, often atonal amalgam of oppressing sounds and vengeful atmospheres: but where Lou Reed, Psychic TV and Public Image Limited made industrial music a dismally unattractive noise aimed directly at the bedsit depressive in all of us, Reznor managed to turn it around in the Nineties by injecting some good old-fashioned sex back into the recipe. Without Nine Inch Nails there would be no Marilyn Manson or Orgy, and the music of Korn, Slipknot and Coal Chamber would sound markedly different.

The first NIN album was 1989's *Pretty Hate Machine*, which was the first album of its kind to appeal to mainstream rock audiences, due to Reznor's strung-out, high-cheekboned pout and his use of classic pop song structures underneath the clanking industrial sounds. The relentless self-hatred and paranoia that pervaded both lyrics and music made it dark enough for even the gloomiest of rock fans, and it sold by the truckload. The album remained on the American charts for a remarkable three years after its release.

Reznor assembled a touring band for 1991's first Lollapalooza tour and refined the act to anarchic proportions: more and more fans gathered but, frustratingly, legal problems between the composer and his record company prevented any new material from appearing. A ferocious EP, *Broken*, appeared in 1992, but a full-length album didn't appear until 1994: however, it seemed that the wait had been worthwhile. The five-million-selling *The Downward*

Spiral was a progressive album (King Crimson guitarist Adrian Belew made a memorable guest contribution) which attracted a new generation of fans wise to classic Seventies rock and who had heard of Reznor due to his groundbreaking work on the soundtrack of Oliver Stone's *Natural Born Killers*, which had won several awards. And with good reason, too – Reznor had managed to combine snatches of dialogue from the film with music as diverse as thrash metal (Lard) and folk-rock (Bob Dylan): no mean feat by anybody's standards.

In the face of all this adulation, Reznor kept himself busy by founding a record label, Nothing, performing at Woodstock 94, producing or executive-producing albums by Marilyn Manson, managing another soundtrack (this time for David Lynch's *Lost Highway*), issuing a video collection, *Closure*, and composing music for the cult computer game *Quake*.

1999's *The Fragile* album – a mighty 23 tracks of music covering almost two hours – was another enormous success, taking Trent two years to record and leading to accolades such as 'One of the most influential people in America' and 'The most vital artist in music today' from the music press. Finally, Reznor followed in the footsteps of Fear Factory and released a remix album the following year: *Things Falling Apart* was a logical complement to his heavily electronic work and featured high-quality retweaks from console-masters of the calibre of Adrian Sherwood.

The music of Nine Inch Nails isn't for everyone – but its leader's status as a true innovator cannot be disputed.

NINE INCH NAILS: Responsible for the darker side of nu-metal

NONPOINT

www.nonpoint.com

Leading players in the Spanish rap-metal movement, Nonpoint come from Florida and gained their name from Nonpoint Factor, the band that New York-born drummer Robb Rivera led in Puerto Rico before re-crossing the border. His bandmate, singer Elias Soriano, is also a Puerto Rican and raps both in Spanish and English. The other Nonpoint players are the Americans Andrew Goldman (guitar) and KB (bass), both originally from the band Fuse.

The foursome discovered a cohesion previously unprecedented in Latinocore bands on their formation in Miami in 1997, and rapidly developed a powerful,

Statement, which appeared in 2000. It featured a Spanish-language anthem, 'Orgullo' (meaning 'pride'), a hip-hop workout called 'Double Stacked' and a rap marathon with Darwin's Waiting Room speed-talker Grimm, entitled 'Tribute'. A hit on the local metal scene, *Statement* made Nonpoint a festival regular.

NOTHINGFACE

www.nothingface.com

A band from Washington DC which mixes traditional rock and even some pop melodies into its particular metallic brew, Nothingface was formed in 1995 by Matt Holt (vocals), Tom Maxwell (guitar), Bill Gaal (bass) and Chris Houck (drums). The local label DCide released two

NONPOINT: Hasta la vista, hombres!

crushing sound, despite the commercial demands of the dance-based Miami music scene. An independent album, *Separate Yourself*, appeared later that year and was followed by *Struggle*, released on the Jugular label in 1999.

However, it was a signing to the giant MCA label that propelled Nonpoint into the wider arena with their third album

Nothingface recordings, *Pacifier* (1997) and *An Audio Guide To Everyday Atrocity* (1998) before the TVT organisation stepped up with a deal, leading to the *Violence* album in 2000. Received by the nation's punk and metal fans with more or less equal enthusiasm, the band began to tour, apparently unhindered by the replacement of Houck and Gaal by Tommy Sickles and ex-Deadlights four-stringer Jerry Montano.

ONE MINUTE SILENCE

www.oneminutesilence.net

An extremely powerful live act drawing its energy from an agenda including anti-racist and anti-capitalist themes, the English-Irish One Minute Silence are made up of the almost insanely driven singer Brian 'Yap' Barry, guitarist Chris Ignatiou, bassist Glenn Diani and drummer Eddie Stratton. The band were originally named Near Death Experience but were obliged to change the moniker after discovering the existence of not one, but two bands gigging

under the same name. An indie deal with the esoteric Big Cat label produced the *Available In All Colours* album in 1998, which was acclaimed by the press, before the recruitment of another guitarist, the youthful but frighteningly talented Massy.

It wasn't long before the band's extensive appearances on the London club scene attracted major-label interest, and it was ultimately V2 who secured the OMS signature on a contract. The first fruits of this partnership was *Buy Now... Saved Later*, produced by Machine Head/Fear Factory veteran Colin Richardson and released in April 2000. This was a notable departure for One Minute Silence, whose debut had been produced by hip-hop console twiddler Machine – and possibly the band's deliberate response to the growing homogeneity of the rap-rock sound.

Tours with Sevendust, Godsmack, Sepultura, Anthrax and Biohazard have all seen the OMS live presence grow, and the band look set to join the upper ranks of nu-metal in the coming months, provided that the kids can stomach their relatively serious message.

ORGY: The new faces of glam-metal

ORGY

www.orgymusic.com

A brushed-up, shiny new version of Nine Inch Nails, LA's Orgy produces music that centres on the usual blinding riffs but with unashamedly poppy hooks, melodies and choruses, leading to the label 'death-pop' – God knows which bored journalist thought that one up, but it does seem to capture the band's glittery, post-millennial sound effectively.

Orgy first assembled in 1997. Its members – Jay Gordon (vocals), Ryan Shuck (guitar), Amir Derakh (guitar synth), Paige Haley (bass) and Bobby Hewitt (drums) – were all experienced in the workings of the West Coast music scene: Shuck in particular had collaborated with Korn singer Jonathan Davis, while Derakh had been a local producer for some years. When Bakersfield's most famous ex-residents Korn struck it lucky and founded a record label, Elementree, its first signing was Orgy.

An album, *Candyass*, was released in 1998 and was a Californian success, due in part to the convincingly futuristic sound of the band (Derakh's guitar synth came in handy here), although Gordon later called it "a bunch of lies and fairy tales". A spot on the first Family Values tour saw Orgy develop a finely-honed live act and many of Korn's enormous fanbase gravitated towards them. The follow-up album, *Vapor Transmission*, was released two years later and continued along even more sci-fi lines, including a fully-fledged cyberpunk (I use the word advisedly – in its dated early-Nineties sense) vision of the future in the song 'The Odyssey'.

Whether or not such imagery becomes old-fashioned (and such things can happen very rapidly) will determine Orgy's future. Remember what happened to Sigue Sigue Sputnik?

PAPA ROACH

www.paparoach.com

Like their junior brethren Linkin Park, North California's Papa Roach have been accused – by the more small-minded members of the music press, at least – of peddling deliberately chart-oriented music rather than pursuing the true spirit of metal, whatever that may be. This is largely due to the unexpected success of a couple of singles in 2000, both inoffensive

PAPA ROACH: Like the Insect they're named after, it's hard to escape this bunch.

nu-metal-by-numbers helpings of angst and moderately heavy riffing. The fact that the band wear only black makes the sniggers even louder.

However, let's leave snideness to those who enjoy it and look more closely at the band's roots. They have a surprising amount of history, being formed in 1993, a full seven years before even troubling the charts. Coby Dick (vocals), Jerry Horton (guitar), Will James (bass – replaced in 1996 by Tobin Esperance) and Dave Buckner (drums) began recording and releasing EPs on their own New Noize label, none of which did especially frantic business in the era of grunge and alternative radio rock. Some of the album titles served as pointers towards the patented Roach sense of humour (*Potatoes For Christmas, Caca Bonita* and so on), but despite all the gauche foolishness a reputation began to grow, and when the band got round to releasing a fully-fledged album, *Old Friends From Young Years*, sales were sufficient to make it a local radio hit. Tours with Powerman 5000, Sevendust and the evergreen old-faithfuls Suicidal Tendencies ensued and a label war of sorts ensued, with the newly-formed Dreamworks Records as the winner.

Serious success beckoned with the release of *Infest* in 2000. By this time a professional image and sound had been achieved and, with the impact of the 'Last Resort' single (kids loved its "Cut my life into pieces!" hook), the status of the Roach at the top of the *new* nu-metal tree was assured.

But when any band's rise to prominence is based on just one or two songs, it's a precarious situation: there are only so many times a song can be played before it starts to grate, and given that Papa Roach seemed to have irked more than their fair share of rock journalists through no fault of their own, a slippery slide into third-album obscurity is a genuine risk. Let us hope they share the uncanny survival skills of their unhygienic, six-legged namesakes.

PAYABLE ON DEATH

www.payableondeath.com

Cynics might suggest that Payable On Death have made a unique selling point out of their publicly-professed Christianity, or even that their faith is a complete invention designed to attract the more timid metal fan. More charitable individuals might applaud the band for their honesty and courage. However, most of us will simply wince at the memory of hideous 'Christian metal' bands from the Eighties like the appalling Stryper, whose squeaky-clean hair-metal (*To Hell With The Devil* was just one of their catchier album titles) was set off perfectly by a vile black and yellow stripe theme. And now we've got a Christian nu-metal band. Can times really have changed so much that the church and metal are able to co-exist credibly?

It would appear so. POD have, it seems, lived a genuinely tough life, and take their worship seriously. Forming in 1992, their career was a slog for six long years until Atlantic signed them up in August 1998: singer Sonny, guitarist Marcos, original Cleveland resident and bassist Tra_ (yes, it *is* spelled like that) and drummer Wuv came straight from the mean streets of San Diego. Wuv's father, the drummer claims, was a successful drug dealer until he saw the light, while it was the death of Sonny's mother from cancer which brought God into his life.

Neighbourhood house parties were the first POD live outings, but it wasn't long until the band were self-releasing albums on their own Rescue Records label and supporting Green Day. In fact, three long-players were recorded and issued – the last of which, *Brown*, sold an amazing 30,000 copies – before Atlantic became involved: an incredible achievement for a young band from the ghetto, divine assistance or not.

Local shows supporting ska-metallers Mighty Mighty Bosstones, dope-hoppers Cypress Hill and Pennywise followed, and a gruelling 150-gigs-per-year schedule took shape, with the help of a group of dedicated followers, the POD Warriors. The band does a lot of charity gigs, which helps to explain its grass-roots popularity.

So it seems that Christian metal is still a viable concept after all. God help us.

PIST.ON

New York nu-metallers Pist.On debuted in 1996 with the ferocious (and ironically-titled) *Number One*, which was noted for the power of the rhythm section – bassist and backup singer Val Ium is also something of a metaller's pin-up – and the melodies created by singer and composer Henry Font. The other Pist.Ons were

initially guitarist Paul Poulos and drummer Danny Jam Kavadlo, but both departed the following year.

Returning with a new line-up in 1999 – guitarist Burton Gans and drummer Jeff McManus had been recruited – and a new album, *Sell Out*, the band became favourites of the rock press, and seem set for further successes.

PIST.ON: Darlings of the metal press

PITCHSHIFTER

www.pitchshifter.com

As much a drum'n'bass or techno outfit as a nu-metal band, the UK's Pitchshifter is one of those rare acts whose music is almost impossible to label. Few other groups are as confrontational: imagine the Prodigy at their 1997 peak, but with a much harder, sharper sound and look and you're approaching the right image.

Formed in the early Nineties by the Clayden brothers (J.S. the singer and programmer, M.D. the bass player) with J.A. Carter on guitar and simply D. on live drums, the early Pitchshifter obsessions were technology (a pitchshifter is the modulation control on a synthesiser or, more currently, a feature of a music-editing program), the ethics of punk and the compressed gloom of industrial rock. Combining these elements to make as fearsome a racket as possible was the Pitchshifter agenda from day one.

The progressive Earache label signed the band in 1992, and it was in America that the PS sound made most immediate headway. An 1992 EP, *Submit*, and the debut album of a year later, *Psensitised*, conveyed the band's chaotic message without any room for misinterpretation, and a space was made on the industrial underground (a dark, violent place far removed from your mainstream club scene, in case you were wondering) for Pitchshifter.

Live shows involved spontaneous live programming, creating a visceral, ever-shifting sound barrage, which was complemented (or if you prefer, exacerbated) by the eyeball-searing visuals projected onto the walls. The brain-shafting Pitchshifter experience was taken a level higher by a remix album, *Pitchshifter Vs... The Remix Wars*, released in 1995 and containing a set of PS songs retweaked by

the press almost as revolutionaries – largely because they had chosen to include a batch of free samples at the end of the CD, and encouraged the fans to use these for their own purposes.

Tours with the aforementioned Ministry, Tool and Korn kept public awareness high Stateside and after a label switch to DGC, a long-player entitled *www.pitchshifter.com* was released. The title – now a little obsolete, as high-tech concepts go – was novel at the time, and the concept of Pitchshifter as cyber-guerillas rapidly spread. The hip-hop producer Machine said at the time that the aim was to make the "sickest, most ultimate guitar-dance music crossover record imaginable" – an objective

PITCHSHIFTER: A fearsome racket

various knob-twiddlers. The band themselves were soon asked to return the favour for industrial monoliths such as Ministry. The year was also notable for the appearance of a corn-circle, suspiciously similar to the PS logo in shape, in a field next to the Phoenix Festival, where the band were playing – well, it *was* a topical subject at the time...

The 1996 album *Infotainment* was more subtle, retaining most of the naked aggression but refining the sound with a more exploratory approach. The band were labelled by the more excitable members of

which most would agree was achieved. This was reinforced by *Deviant*, released in summer 2000, and JS's adoption of all-white contact lenses for that all-important child-scaring Marilyn Manson look.

The singer has gone on to label his music 'strum'n'bass', for anyone who needs a category, but Pitchshifter's ever-innovative work makes them one of the few bands in this book whose music simply cannot be defined. A Shifter gig remains a frantic, frightening, exhilarating ride. Their recent split with their record label will hopefully be a mere glitch in their fortunes: long may they make their unique racket.

POWERMAN 5000

http://powermantest.artistdirect.com

A cult underground act on the point of breaking through, the Boston-by-birth, California-by-choice Powerman 5000 were formed in 1994 when the central members, Spider One (vocals) and M33 (guitar) met at the Berklee Music School. The former is the brother of dreadlocked metal vagrant Rob Zombie, while M33's brother John Tempesta also plays guitar in Zombie's band.

A debut album, 1995's *The Blood Splat Rating System*, was issued by the Conscience label and encouraged a Boston fanbase to

PRIMUS

www.primussucks.com

O ne of the strangest bands in this book, San Francisco's Primus have appealed to all sectors of the metal-buying audience since their inception in 1984: alternative fans enjoy their almost perverse unpredictability and their willingness to experiment with many styles of music, while metalheads love them for their considerable power, and even jazz and blues fans admire their jaw-dropping musical dexterity.

Primus centres on the phenomenal bass guitar skills of sometime Blind Illusion

POWERMAN 5000: Come back Billy Idol! All is forgiven!

accumulate, boosted by the release two years later of *Mega Kung Fu Radio* on Dreamworks. Although the second album was basically a remix of the first, fans remained keen, and a third long-player, *Tonight The Stars Revolt*, kept the PM 5000 profile healthy. They remain a popular C-league metal act.

player Les Claypool, who first put the band together with guitarist Todd Huth and the first of a succession of seven drummers. However, Huth was soon replaced by the nimble-plectrummed guitarist Larry Lalonde, a sometime student of six- (and seven-) string guru Joe Satriani and, bizarrely, an ex-member of the pioneering death metal band Possessed. Immediately hitting on a weird mixture of metal, jazz, punk, rap and funk, Claypool described his band's sound as 'psychedelic polka' and - for reasons best known to themselves - Primus began composing tunes referring to sea life. Honestly: their label was called Prawn Song, which released a debut album, *Suck On This*, in 1989.

A San Fran compilation, *Frizzle Fry*, featured some Primus tracks and went on to win a Bay Area Music Award. Tours with similarly quirky bands such as Jane's Addiction, Living Colour and the grandaddies of weirdcore, Faith No More, bolstered their profile and a deal was signed with the Interscope label. Primus' activities then began to proliferate, with an album, the Monty Python-esque *Sailing The Seas Of Cheese*, released the following year and a single, 'Tommy The Cat' (featuring Tom Waits on guest vocals) selected for the *Bill And Ted's Bogus Journey* soundtrack. The band also briefly appeared in the movie, as did Jim Martin of Faith No More.

Support slots with luminaries outside the metal world such as the evergreen Canadians Rush followed. A notable jaunt took place with U2, who were approaching the end of their lantern-jawed, socially-concerned *Rattle & Hum* period and apparently wanted to demonstrate that they still had a sense of humour.

But it was the newly-formed Lollapalooza tour, which took Primus on board in 1993, which became their true spiritual home. The headline slot led to the success of the *Pork Soda* album and its lead-off single, 'My Name Is Mud', which made it to No. 7 on the US singles chart. The ever-restless Claypool also formed a side-project, Sausage, with the original Primus axeman Huth and a drummer, Jay Lane, recording the *Riddles Are Abound Tonight* album in 1994.

The next Primus long-player, 1995's *Tales From The Punch Bowl*, included a novelty hit, 'Wynona's Big Brown Beaver', and was received with rapture by a new generation of teenage fans. Claypool released a solo album in 1996 to less acclaim (not that the public's reception has ever affected the work or the morale of this oddest of bands) and filled in time before touring once more by recruiting ex-Godflesh drummer Brian Mantia to replace Alexander, who had departed.

The cult American animated series *South Park* provided Primus with the perfect soundtrack opportunity, and the Claypool-authored theme tune has become one of their best-known songs: meanwhile, 1997's *The Brown Album* kept things at a suitably trivial level. Just in case anybody thought that Primus had gone serious, however, the *Rhinoplasty* EP - featuring covers of songs by the Police, Peter Gabriel and Metallica - was an anarchic record, causinng many a furrowed brow at the musical antics it contained.

1999's *Antipop* was the album that long-standing fans had dreaded - a jokes-apart, let's-play-properly record. Unusually, Primus had recruited a different producer for almost every song: those invited to man the desk included Limp Bizkit's Fred Durst, *South Park* creator Matt Stone, Police drummer Stewart Copeland, Rage Against the Machine's Tom Morello and the old growler Tom Waits. The album also featured

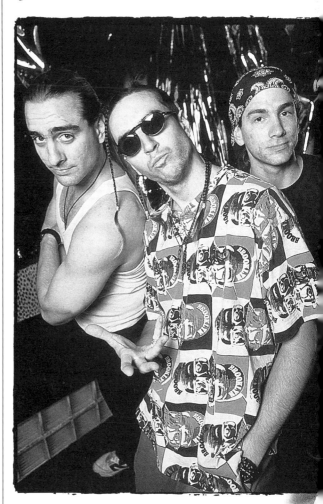

PRIMUS: Very cool, but *very* strange

musical contributions by heavyweight axe-wielders James Hetfield of Metallica and the aforementioned Faith No More guitarist Jim Martin.

2000 appeared to be the beginning of an extended break for Primus: Mantia left to join the new Guns N'Roses line-up and Claypool announced that activities would cease for the foreseeable future. Les himself was far from inactive, however, recording an album with another band, Oyster Head (featuring Stewart Copeland and Phish guitarist Trey Anastasio) and two solo sets, *Live Frogs 1* and *2*.

Latest Primus news includes the rumour that Claypool was set to join his old friends Metallica after the departure of bassist Jason Newsted left them a man short in summer 2001. He had originally been tentatively mooted to join the seminal thrash-metallers when Newsted's predecessor, the remarkable Cliff Burton, was tragically killed back in 1986. However, the rumour appears to be just that, and in any case Claypool's legacy is the multifaceted body of work which Primus have produced over almost two decades. And he'll be back - a pioneer like this doesn't stay down for long.

PROFESSIONAL MURDER MUSIC

Another hard-hitting industrial metal band, LA's grimly-titled Professional Murder Music consists of Roman Marisak (vocals, guitar, keyboards), Jeff Schartoff (bass, keyboards), Brian Harrah (guitar) and Justin Bennett (drums). Marisak and Schartoff knew each other from their previous band, Human Waste Project, while Harrah had been a member of Tura Satana (featuring Tairrie B, now of My Ruin, on vocals), with whom Human Waste Project had toured. When both bands split, the three musicians recruited Bennett on drums and formed their own project.

After taking the bold decision to record an EP and release it over the internet, PMM embarked on a gruelling tour schedule with bands as disparate as Kid Rock, Fear Factory, Powerman 5000, Orgy and Static-X, and were pleasantly surprised to see that many of the fans they encountered knew them already from their previous two bands. A single, 'Slow'

(produced by sometime Metallica and Alice In Chains studio bod Toby Wright) was snapped up and found itself on the soundtrack to *End Of Days*, a mediocre 1999 film in which Arnold Schwarzenegger plays an alcoholic copper who takes on the devil.

Evidently sensing the PMM potential, Geffen signed the band. Their self-titled debut was produced by Josh Abraham, who had also produced albums by Orgy and Powerman 5000. PMM then appeared on the Tattoo The Earth tour with a powerful line-up that included Slayer, and watched the album's sales figures rise: one of the reasons for its success were the memorable cameos by A Perfect Circle guitarist Troy Van Leeuwen on 'Fall Again' and sometime Mötley Crüe drummer Tommy Lee on an as-yet-unreleased tune, 'Disconnect'. Former Human Waste Project singer Aimee Echo also guests on 'Does It Dream', while an unexpected appearance is made by Limp Bizkit's DJ Lethal on 'Painkiller Intro'.

And that name? Schartoff shrugs off any violent or misanthropic accusations: "I mean, would you ask Korn if they like it on the cob or creamed? Likewise, it's silly to assume that we dig serial killers. Our name [is] more a statement of how we feel that much of pop music is contrived crap." You read it here first.

PUDDLE OF MUDD

www.puddleofmudd.com

Like Staind before them, Kansas City's Puddle Of Mudd (first formed in 1993) were brought to the public's attention by a certain Fred Durst, who came to hear of them when singer/guitarist Wes Scantlin attended the second Family Values tour and handed his band's demo tape to Durst's security guard during Limp Bizkit's set. As the Bizkit singer receives dozens of similar recordings on a daily basis, Scantlin wasn't optimistic about getting a reply – and was duly surprised when the phone rang a couple of weeks later.

Durst was keen on the band, and especially Scantlin's powerful, melodic vocals. In an ironic twist, the first line-up of Puddle Of Mudd had drifted apart just before Fred's phone call, and all Wes's frantic attempts to reunite them proved to be of no avail. However, Durst proved to be willing to compromise and flew Scantlin to

Los Angeles, where he promised to find musicians for a new line-up.

Once in LA, Wes and Fred auditioned a bevy of aspiring nu-metallers and ultimately recruited ex-Happy Hour guitarist Paul Phillips (a friend of Fred's from Jacksonville), Interscope employee, bassist and ex-Cellophane four-stringer Douglas Ardito and Chris Cornell drummer Greg Upchurch (recruited later after sometime Guns N'Roses/A Perfect Circle sticksman Josh Freese temporarily sat in). Fred signed the band to his Flawless label, songwriting sessions commenced and an album, *Come*

PULKAS

www.earache.com

A typically eardrum-shafting Earache signing, Londoners Pulkas first met while travelling on the tube in 1995 and the line-up (vocalist Luke Lloyd, guitarist Martin Bourne, bassist Jules McBride and drummer Rob Lewis) set about recording a demo. The songs 'This Is It' and 'Control' impressed the Nottingham label enough for a deal to be offered, although the band had played fewer than a dozen gigs by the time the signing occurred.

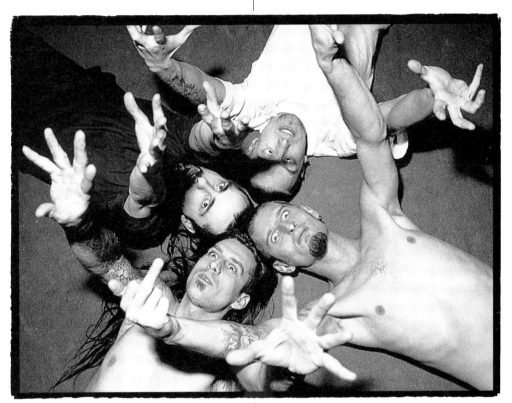

PULKAS: The new generation of ear-bleeding electronic metal

Clean, was recorded, a mixture of POM's pre-Durst material and newer songs.

Also like Staind, the first album was a colossal success in summer 2001, selling over 100,000 copies in a matter of weeks. And that name? Scantlin explains it as the result of a flooded practice room back in Kansas City many years before – the Missouri River had broken its banks, poured into the rehearsal room and left the floor one giant swamp.

Gathering some of its most hard-hitting acts, Earache assembled the NextGen tour in 1998, featuring Pulkas on a bill with Misery Loves Co, Dub War and Janus Stark, before recruiting renowned producer Colin Richardson (of Machine Head and Fear Factory fame) to produce Pulkas' first album.

The result, *Greed*, was taken on the road through Belgium, Spain and Britain and caused one or two raised eyebrows for its cover, a depiction of a sperm burrowing into an egg. It could have been worse, surely?

Q

QUEENS OF THE STONE AGE

www.qotsa.com

Straddling the unclassifiable area that lies between nu-metal, doom metal, stoner rock and psychedelia, Queens Of The Stone Age turned many a head in 2000 for their sudden ascendance into the pop charts of the world. It's difficult to say what propelled their rise to the public eye: the principal band-members had served time in bands of cult interest, it's true, but none of them could be described as runaway successes. QOTSA's rise to glory has been one of the clearest signs yet that the music-buying public has become more metallic in its tastes.

In the first half of the Nineties, stoner rock was the province of Kyuss, who spent several profitable years building a reputation for their sparse, evocative desert tunes before abruptly imploding in 1995. Singer and guitarist Josh Homme then moved from the Californian hinterlands to Seattle and hooked up with the Screaming Trees, with whom he played live and sporadically recorded. After a time, a loose group of musicians had gathered, among them Soundgarden's Matt Cameron, Dinosaur Jr.'s Mike Johnson and various members of the Trees themselves. Haphazardly organised by Homme, a series of singles were recorded under the name Gamma Ray (not under any circumstances to be confused with the German power metal outfit of the same name). He also assembled tracks for a sequence of six albums, referred to collectively as *The Desert Sessions*.

Homme then put together a more permanent band, including Kyuss drummer Alfredo Hernandez, a second guitarist and keyboard player, Dave Catching, and the insane Kyuss bassist Nick Oliveri, whose permanent hedonism, memorable facial hair and penchant for performing nude make him one of the more unusual – and appealing – characters in modern rock. Oliveri had been dividing his time since the demise of Kyuss between the deranged punk band the Dwarves (under the name Rex Everything) and his side project, Mondo Generator.

Homme christened the new band Queens Of The Stone Age to spite the redneck rockers he saw coming to Kyuss gigs: "It'll be interesting if they can say the name to their friends," he sniggered.

QUEENS OF THE STONE AGE: Bringing drug-laden desert songs to the masses

QOTSA's Nick Olieri

The self-titled debut album, a deft, economical blend of alternative rock and metal, attracted fans immediately and was issued in 1998 by the Loosegroove label to moderate local acclaim. *Rolling Stone* even named QOTSA one of the 'Ten Most Important Hard and Heavy Bands Right Now' in a yearly poll.

However, the band might have remained a minor-league act if Homme hadn't managed to pull two perfect pop-metal singles out of the bag. 'Feelgood Hit Of The Summer', with its recited list of stimulants legal and otherwise, and 'The Lost Art Of Keeping A Secret', a kind of dark anthem, saw the Queens hit high on charts worldwide and the associated album, *Rated R*, rapidly went platinum. Tours with Bad Religion, the Smashing Pumpkins and Hole helped matters along and the band were even featured in mainstream pop press. 2001 has been quieter for QOTSA, but it's only a matter of time before they're back, it is predicted.

A story that no-one could have foreseen, then. Ten years ago, a band like the Queens would have struggled to fill clubs: now they pack stadiums. It's a funny old world.

RAGE AGAINST THE MACHINE

www.ratm.com

Not only the most politically outspoken and active band in this book, but in the entire pantheon of heavy metal, Rage Against The Machine have never stopped trying to get their message across. Only the most extreme punk bands (Conflict and the Dead Kennedys were notable examples) ever matched the intensity of their polemic. The target of all this wrath is, quite simply, the whole of Western society: in RATM's eyes, this is a pretty poor place to live. The world is run by profiteering capitalists, they state; the media is in hock to the corporations who exploit the planet's poorer nations as cattle for profit, while soothing the fat, rich West into a dull, manipulable stupor; we are all slaves to mind control; stupidity and hypocrisy are the whole of our laws; and we are all doomed to be exploited and die in infantile ignorance at the hands of the military-industrial complex. And Rage are here to spread the word, with a ferocious mixture of rapping and riffing. Heavy going, in all senses.

It's fair to say that Faith No More invented rap-metal, and Korn were the first real nu-metallers. But Rage Against The Machine are the missing link between the two, with crisp, disciplined guitar figures supporting vitriolic whispered, intoned or bellowed invective. The former comes from six-stringer Tom Morello, who had honed his playing with the hardcore band Lock Up; he is also the nephew of the first Kenyan president, Jomo Kenyatta. The spoken-word content is provided courtesy of the dreadlocked pin-up Zack de la Rocha, an almost frighteningly committed individual whose father Beto is a well-known political artist. The other RATM musicians are Tim Commerford (bass) and sometime Eddie Vedder collaborator Brad Wilk (drums), an apparently more introverted pair than the guitarist and vocalist: although Commerford displayed some signs of instability in 2000, as we shall see, and makes even hardened metallers wince at the sight of his tattoos – blocks of colour that obscure most of his arms and legs. None of your screaming skulls and British bulldogs here – his skin art is *completely* solid. Ouch.

The band was formed in 1991 in Los Angeles after the split of their earlier groups, and quickly wrote and recorded a 12-track demo tape. This featured one of their best-known songs, 'Bullet In The Head': an early call to wakefulness, with de la Rocha addressing mass apathy with the sneering accusation "Believing all the lies that they're telling you/Buying all the products that they're selling you!" The demo (which went on to sell over 5,000 copies) persuaded no less an organisation than Epic Records to sign them, a move that led to some derision from the band's local fanbase: Epic, a subsidiary of the mighty Sony corporation, was the very 'machine' of the band's name, and some of the hardcore faithful believed that the signing represented a sell-out. Not so, responded the band: a powerful platform was required if the RATM message was to be disseminated effectively.

In July 1992 Rage supported the first show by Porno For Pyros, the new incarnation of ex-Jane's Addiction frontman Perry Farrell. This was an important gig to be seen at, with the cream of LA's media players present – and the band's slamming

performance went down a storm. In November they played on Farrell's new Lollapalooza tour before travelling to Europe in support of veteran hardcore act Suicidal Tendencies.

Rage's self-titled debut album – probably the most influential recording listed in this volume – was released on November 6, 1992, and became an instant classic. With its intimidating opener, 'Bombtrack', and the apocalyptic death-knells of 'Bullet In The Head' and 'Know Your Enemy', it was a feral, exciting record, and spawned two bona fide all-time classics. The first, the anti-KKK 'Killing In The Name', hit fans hard in the pit of the stomach with its famous downtuned riff and has inspired countless venue audiences to anarchy with its simple repeated scream of "Fuck you, I won't do what you tell me!" The other, the equally effective 'Freedom', asked the listener, "Why stand on a silent platform?/Fight the law!/Fuck the norm!". Both songs were simple, deadly calls-to-arms, and the world's metal-buying teenagers bought the album as fast as Epic could press copies.

After a tour with House Of Pain in March 1993 and a few months of preparation, Rage grabbed headlines in July with their appearance on the third Lollapalooza tour by walking on-stage naked (except for PMRC painted on their

RAGE AGAINST THE MACHINE:
Probably didn't vote for Bush

chests and their mouths sealed with duct tape) and standing, sullen and silent, for a full fifteen minutes. The message was clear, although the impression on Tipper Gore and her right-wing cronies at the Parents' Music Resource Center – an American organisation dedicated to warning buyers against shocking, violent or otherwise undesirable lyrics in music – is not known.

A headline spot at an Anti-Nazi League benefit show at London's Brixton Academy, plus tours with Cypress Hill, saw out the rest of 1993, while a concert in aid of political prisoner Leonard Peltier took place in April 1994, raising over $75,000 for Peltier's defence fund. A similar event, dubbed 'Latinpalooza', took place in October. The band then took some time out to recover and record a second album, although another benefit show, this time for Mumia Abu-Jamal, a journalist imprisoned for the supposed murder of a police officer, was held in August 1995.

The extended wait between albums was starting to become irksome for America's metal fans – who had, after all, now got Korn to play with – but RATM stayed in the news in April 1996, when their set on NBC's *Saturday Night Live* was truncated when they attempted to hang the American flag upside down from their amplifiers. Just in time for the impatient fans came the release of *Evil Empire* three days later, which entered the US album charts at No. 1 and provided hit singles with 'Bulls On Parade' and the inspired 'People Of The Sun'. The album's inner sleeve also featured a veritable revolutionary's library of radical texts, all of which can be seen at the Rage website to this day.

In January 1997 a special Radio Free LA concert took place, featuring a band composed of Morello, de la Rocha, Flea of the Red Hot Chili Peppers on bass and Porno For Pyros drummer Steven Perkins. The broadcast also featured Beck and Cypress Hill.

After tours with U2 and Wu-Tang Clan, Morello caused headlines by being arrested at a March Of Conscience rally against the Guess company, which allegedly uses sweatshop labour in Asia during the manufacture of its products.

May 1999 saw a Rage track, 'No Shelter', appear on the *Godzilla* soundtrack and receive a nomination for Best Metal Performance at the 40th Annual Grammy Awards, while towards the end of the year

Zack spoke before a session of the International Commission of Human Rights at the United Nations in Geneva about the incarceration of Mumia Abu-Jamal and American capital punishment laws.

Album number three – targeted closer to home, with the title *The Battle Of Los Angeles* – was released in late 1999 and, like its predecessor, entered the charts at the top spot and went platinum in a matter of months. However, it seemed that Rage's momentum had deserted them to a certain extent: perhaps the public had tired of their relentless activism. Whatever the truth, something seemed to snap in bassist Commerford; during a performance by saccharine moppet Britney Spears of The Rolling Stones' 'Satisfaction' at the MTV Video Music Awards in 2000, he lost all patience and started to climb a 15-foot-high column that formed part of the set. Reaching the top, he started trying to rock the structure in order to break it, much to the amused concern of Limp Bizkit's Fred Durst, who was accepting an award at the time. Eventually security guards got him down and, with a certain amount of fisticuffs, ejected him from the venue. Although this anarchic gesture might have seemed perfect for Rage Against The Machine, in fact all was not well: "I was so humiliated," said de la Rocha, "that I went home".

Shortly afterwards, despite Morello's promises of a live Rage album, Zack announced his departure from the band. The remaining three stated that RATM would not split and that the singer's move was entirely amicable, although de la Rocha blamed "breakdowns in communication and group decision-making" for his decision. In December 2000 a covers album, *Renegades*, was released, featuring takes on work by artists as diverse as Devo, Bruce Springsteen and Afrika Bambaataa. However, most fans perceived it as a stop-gap release and it sold only moderately well.

All of which brings the Rage story up to date. Rumour has it that Zack's replacement might be none other than ex-Soundgarden singer Chris Cornell, although this is looking increasingly unlikely as time passes. What is certain is that both de la Rocha and his compadres will return in some form or other. Passion of this calibre is rare in any medium, and usually impossible to repress for very long.

RAGING SPEEDHORN

www.ragingspeedhorn.co.uk

The leading UK proponent of what could be termed 'extreme nu-metal' – i.e. a combination of the funky beats of the modern style combined with death and thrash metal – is Raging Speedhorn, an alarmingly youthful band from Corby in Northamptonshire. Like Slipknot before them, the fact that their home town can be a fairly grim place in which to grow up (the town's steel industry collapsed in the Seventies, leading to a generation of unemployment) has informed the band's work with an easily-recognisable touch of wrath.

Formed in August 1998 from two Corby bands, Box and Soulcellar, the band have made their name through constant live appearances, appearing with a plethora of bands of all stripes. Perhaps because of their allegiance to both extreme and nu-metal, they've been able to support thrash metallers (Testament, Anal Cunt), punk acts (Snapcase), industrial rockers (Ministry), stoner rock bands (Karma To Burn, Iron Monkey) and the cream of the nu crop (they opened 2001's Ozzfest with Slipknot and Soulfly).

The RS name was first brought to the public's attention in 1999 when they released a demo, recorded with Cubanate guitarist Roddy Stone, which sold 800 copies. Tracks from the tape were included on compilations ('Knives And Faces' on the

RAGING SPEEDHORN: The band most likely to pioneer 'extreme nu-metal'

Raging Speedhorn has two vocalists, Frank Regan and John Loughlin, who cover the throatal spectrum with death metal roars, sinister whispered moments, pure old-school raps and even standard rock melodies. Together with guitarists Gareth Smith and Tony Loughlin, bassist Darren Smith and drummer Gordon Morrison, the Speedhorn live presence is a powerful one, made more convincing by the fact that the members look like they've just walked off the street – there's no make-up or futuristic uniform here.

Org label, and 'Superscud' on a sampler from the rather larger Century Media stable). A third track, the anarchic 'Thumper', made into onto a *Metal Hammer* cover-mount album in December of that year.

2000 was a busy year for Speedhorn, who recorded a second demo in February, supported the now-defunct Iron Monkey and found a manager. With the consistent support of magazines such as *Terrorizer* and *Kerrang!*, more and more fans could be seen wearing the band's infamous Sniff Glue,

Worship Satan T-shirts, and soon enough Speedhorn signed to ZTT and recorded a self-titled debut EP with sometime Nine Inch Nails/Cradle Of Filth producer John Fryer. This became a full-length album after some rethinking, and more gigs were arranged to fill the time before its release. A surprising support slot occurred with Blur guitarist Graham Coxon, a hardcore punk fan who was touring his own solo album in July. This saw Speedhorn playing two nights in front of a largely indie crowd – who did manage, it seems, to get into the music.

The *Raging Speedhorn* album was finally released in February 2001, 2000 copies of which appeared on heavyweight vinyl with signed covers. The success of the single 'The Gush' and more chaotic shows, plus the continued support of the press, has elevated the band to the pinnacle of the British metal scene. It's been a remarkable rise to glory – and the band are only just beginning to hit their stride. The metal of the future starts here.

RAMMSTEIN

www.rammstein.de

One of industrial metal's more innovative bands, Germany's Rammstein has achieved a level of success in recent years that other, more established industrial-mongers – Nine Inch Nails among them – cannot hope to equal. This is due in part to their convincing, competent fusion of grim beats and stamping, anthemic choruses: however, a large part of their popularity must be attributed to the controversy which has surrounded them since their earliest days, usually provided by the more excitable members of the music press.

Like their countrymen Laibach before them, the band has often employed totalitarian imagery to accompany its releases. The slight alarm which this provoked was exacerbated when it was revealed in 1999 that Rammstein's music was among the favourite listening of the students who carried out the killings at the Columbine high school in Colorado. However, the fuss has died down somewhat since then, and the band continue along their own successful path.

Formed in 1994 and consisting of Berlin students Till Lindemann (vocals), Paul Landers (guitar), Richard Kruspe (guitar), Flake Lorenz (keyboards), Oliver Reidel (bass) and Christoph

RAMMSTEIN: A genuinely spooky live experience

Schneider (drums), Rammstein's first work was an album, *Herzeleid*, recorded at the Stockholm Polar studios with Clawfinger producer Jacob Hellner. A single, 'Du Riechst So Gut' was issued in August 1995. Appropriately enough, one version of the single – whose title translates as 'You Smell So Good' – was issued in a limited-edition scented package. The album was released the following month on the German Motor Music label, but sank without making much impact.

Tours with Clawfinger and Project Pitchfork attracted the attention of the media, however, and a second single, 'Seemann', was more successful. A turning-point in the band's fortunes came in the summer of 1996 when the director David Lynch used two songs, 'Heirate Mich' ('Marry Me') and 'Rammstein', on the *Lost Highway* soundtrack. The second album, *Sehnsucht* (meaning *Envy*), was a hit of significant proportions, staying in the German charts for over a year and spawning two memorable hits, 'Engel' and 'Du Hast'. The latter was a popular radio hit worldwide. Late 1997 and early 1998 covers of 'Das Modell' (Kraftwerk) and 'Stripped' (Depeche Mode) also did well, consolidating Rammstein's position near the top of the uneasy-listening tree. For good measure, a revamped version of 'Du Riechst So Gut' was released, featuring remixes by Faith No More and KFMDM.

Mainstream exposure beckoned when Rammstein performed on the 1998 Family Values tour with the nu-metal scene-leaders Korn, Limp Bizkit and Orgy: the presence of ex-NWA rapper Ice Cube also meant that a new audience, the hip-hop crowd, got a taste of Rammstein for the first time. The great and the good of the music industry also opened their eyes to the band at this point, who were nominated for the Best Rock Act award at the MTV European Music Awards in Milan (where they performed 'Du Hast') and at the Grammy ceremony for Best Metal Performance.

1999 saw a somewhat unlikely support slot with pansticked metal ogres Kiss and a live album, *Live Aus Berlin*, which emerged in censored and uncensored versions. The following year was occupied with more tours and the recording of a new album, *Mutter* (the very angst-metal *Mother*), released in spring 2001 after a slot on the ill-fated Big Day Out show in Sydney,

which was marred by the death of a fan during Limp Bizkit's set. The album contained an excellent single, 'Sonne' ('Sun') which was accompanied by a video featuring the band as coal-mining dwarves in service to a sadistic Snow White.

RORSCHACH TEST

www.rorschachtest.com

Named after the psychological test involving the definition of inkblots by subjects, Rorschach Test is an aggressive metal/electronica outfit based around singer James Baker, who formed the band in anger at being expelled from the church. A young priest based in Denver, Colorado, Baker was defrocked in the early Nineties for his allegedly heretical questioning of church doctrine and embarked on a new career as a musician, albeit an annoyed one. Not the usual high-school or college band roots, then.

Recruiting two guitarists, a drummer and a keyboard player, Troee (also from a religious background: his father was a minister), Baker began composing metallic, industrial songs with a definite debt to Ministry and Skinny Puppy but including elements of conventional metal. Gigs in the Denver area were successful and the band decamped for the better prospects of Seattle, just as the grunge scene exploded out of the city into the awareness of music fans worldwide. Some years of local shows and demos followed, while Baker addressed some of the issues that plagued him.

1996 saw the release of an album, *The Eleventh*, which appeared on the band's own label. A second attempt two years later made more of an impact, produced by Neil Kernon (of Queen, Judas Priest and David Bowie fame): *Unclean* spawned a successful single, 'Sex', which received national airplay. Tours with Genitorturers, Ministry, Type O Negative and Korn followed.

A label move to E-Magine Entertainment occurred in late 1999 and another album, *Peace Minus One*, was issued in early 2000 after the re-release of *Unclean*. Line-up changes meant that the band now consisted of Baker, Troee, guitarists Aaron Slip and the ex- N17 player Kris Cannella and drummer Jason Kowalski. They remain a powerful Seattle draw, gaining more exposure now that the grunge movement has been dormant for some time.

S

SALIVA

www.islandrecords.com/saliva

Combining rap, hip-hop, classic rock and metal, Saliva (named after "the glue that holds everything together") are Josey Scott (vocals), Chris Dabaldo (guitar), Wayne Swinny (guitars), Dave Novotny (bass) and Paul Crosby (drums) and hail from the distinctly non-metallic environs of Memphis, Tennessee.

After playing venues on the local music scene for several years, Scott and Dabaldo formed the band in 1996 with the

album – which rapidly sold over 10,000 copies – while the labels were sniffing around.

Eventually Island Records caught up with them after being introduced to their work via a local DJ. A deal was duly inked and the major-label debut, *Every Six Seconds*, appeared in 2001. The record was not titled (as I know many of you are thinking) as a reference to the quite plausible rumour that men think about sex ten times a minute, but after Scott's belief that "life cycles seem to happen every six seconds". A mixture of rap ('Doperide') and old-school riffing ('Click Click Boom'), the album ensured various festival slots that year, while Saliva's appearance alongside Monster Magnet and Slayer on the *Dracula 2000* soundtrack ensured that the Southern flag remained at full mast.

SEGRESSION: Leaders of the Australian pack

intention of combining their favourite styles of music. Their big break came when they won the prestigious National Academy of Recording Arts & Sciences-sponsored Grammy Showcase competition in 1997, a tournament featuring over 6,000 bands from across the USA, and which was intended to uncover the best new unsigned talent in the country. They didn't remain unsigned for long, of course, although they did have time to release an independent

SEGRESSION

www.segression.com.au

An Australian nu-metal band from the far-flung town of Wollongong, Segression are still unsigned at the time of writing but are among the continent's most cutting-edge metal acts. Their first album, *LIA*, was the subject of a handwritten letter of congratulation from Dead Kennedys singer and Alternative Tentacles label head Jello Biafra, while Ozzy Osbourne personally requested their presence as support act when he played down under.

A second album, *Fifth Of The Fifth*, has made Segression the leaders of the Aussie nu-metal scene, and yet no-one has heard of them in the Northern Hemisphere. Perhaps a UK tour is required – after all, it's a bit optimistic to expect most A&R reps to venture south of the Thames, let alone south of the Equator.

SEVEN DUST: Children of the Korn?

SEVENDUST

www.sevendust.com

A deeply heavy band often irksomely compared to Korn and the Deftones, the members of Atlanta's Sevendust (singer Lajon Witherspoon, guitarists Clint Lowery and John Connolly, bassist Vinnie Hornsby and drummer Morgan Rose) first came together in 1995 under the name Crawlspace. After releasing a single, 'My Ruin' – which appeared on the *Mortal Kombat: More Kombat* compilation – the band were obliged to change their name for legal reasons and settled on the mystifying title of Sevendust.

A contract materialised after the band (holding down various McJobs at the time, from gardening to construction) met reps from the TVT label in 1996 at an industry seminar. Having written an album's worth of songs during their two-year stint performing on the Atlanta club scene, it didn't take long for Sevendust to produce an full-length record – like so many debuts in these pages, a self-titled effort – which was released in April 1997. Although sales were initially slow, a Sevendust radio special entitled *Live & Loud* helped push the record and it ultimately went gold in 1998 – coincidentally, on the day that Rose and his girlfriend, Coal Chamber bassist Rayna Foss, found out that they were to have a child.

The second album, *Home*, was produced by Korn/Primus helmsman Toby Wright and featured more of the band's well-known attack, as well as contributions from Deftones frontman Chino Moreno and Skunk Anansie singer Skin. Renowned mixer Andy Wallace added an extra polish to the album and the Dust took it on an extended tour, including spots on the Vans tour and the 2000 Ozzfest.

SHUVEL

www.shuvel.com

Sticking to the Rage Against The Machine rap-riff-scratch template with admirable integrity is Shuvel, from Wichita, Kansas, formed in 1997 and made up of singers Isaac and Jeff Hollinger, guitarist Ryan, bassist Carlos Sandoval and drummer Kyle. The band was formed by the two vocalists, who worked together in various jobs in Wichita before recruiting the other musicians and making the trip out west to Los Angeles.

Rather than demoing by day and playing the Whisky by night – the usual way of attracting A&R reps sniffing out talent – Shuvel secured their deal by playing at a party in San Pedro and falling into conversation with a stripper. The affable girl told them that she had a friend at the Interscope label, and a short while later, after a quick bout of meets'n'greets, a deal was duly signed. Whether the helpful lass received a finder's fee is not known.

Hooking up with 311 producer Scott Ralston, an album was recorded. *Set It Off*, released in 2000, was a thoughtful record, addressing themes such as the Columbine high-school murders of the previous year.

Tours with Kittie and Sevendust ensued, as well as a European jaunt with ex-Mötley Crüe drummer Tommy Lee's new band, Methods Of Mayhem. A Shuvel song appeared on the *Celebrity Deathmatch* soundtrack and the band's name was publicised further thanks to a high-profile appearance on the Ozzfest 2000 festival.

SIKTH

www.sikth.co.uk

Sikth are one of the newest bands in this book, first forming in early 2000 from the ashes of a band boringly called Malpractice, and made their live debut in March at the White Horse in that most underrated of metal havens, High Wycombe. Perhaps Watford's most metallic export, the members of Sikth label their music Skatt-core, although they acknowledge that plenty of hardcore riffs and the odd nu-metal downtuned touch crop up in their tunes.

SKINLAB

www.skinlab1.com

A nu-metal band whose heaviness extends almost as far as the extreme metal genre, Skinlab (now bassist/vocalist Steev Esquivel, guitarists Snake and ex-Killing Culture Scott Sergeant and drummer Paul Hopkins) were formed in San Francisco in late 1995 with the original guitar duo Glen Telford and Gary Wendt. Two demos (the latter of which, *When Pain Comes To Surface*, was produced by the itinerant melodic prog/death metal guitarist James Murphy) persuaded Century Media

SIKTH: An insanely committed live band

Although line-up changes have been impressively frequent, the current two-vocalist set-up (well, it works for Raging Speedhorn and Linkin Park) of ex-Scoured Domain throat-shredder Mikee Goodman and Justin Hill appears stable, and is complemented by guitarists DJ Weller and Mr Pin, bassist James Leach and drummer Dan Foord.

Although they've only produced a single to date (July 2001's frat-boy-humour-titled 'Hold My Finger'), bands of the calibre of One Minute Silence have already paid tribute, and the band's chaotic live antics (one gig, played at high volume above a Porsche showroom, caused the roof to collapse onto the expensive German motors) make them a plausible bet for success.

Records to offer them a deal in 1997 and the band entered the studios with Machine Head, Napalm Death, Earth Crisis and Kreator producer Andy Sneap.

The album, *Bound, Gagged And Blindfolded*, was praised for its punkish power and the band supported it by opening for a host of bands, including Coal Chamber, Exodus, Stuck Mojo and others, through Europe and the US. Wendt and Telford were replaced by Sergeant and Snake and a limited-edition EP, *Eyesore*, was released to keep fans happy until a second album could be completed. It was notable for a cover by the Mexican-American spoof death metal band Brujeria.

Sneap also produced the follow-up,

Disembody: The New Flesh, a tougher, more mature work than earlier recordings, which appeared in 1999 and saw a wider fanbase get the Skinlab bug.

SKRAPE

www.skrape.com

One of the newest of the new nu bands (if you take my meaning) Skrape are a hard-hitting metal act with plenty of hardcore influences and hail from Orlando in Florida. Consisting of vocalist Billy Keeton, guitarists Mike Lynchard and Brian Milner, bassist Pete Sison and drummer Will Hunt, the band built a local following in the metal clubs of the area (which is traditionally home to death metal bands, rather than Skrape's slower, more punkish style) and were signed by RCA in 2000 after performing an industry showcase gig. An album, the very Amen-titled *New Killer America*, was released in 2001 and the band look set to take their approach to the national level.

SLAVES ON DOPE

www.slavesondope.com

Montreal's Slaves On Dope were formed in 1994 as a post-grunge band, but quickly shed the gloomy plaid-shirt approach for a harder, more committed sound and recorded a demo, *Feet*, which rapidly became a local radio favourite. An EP, *Sober*, helped boost the profile further, but the Slaves felt that a Canadian base was not the way forward.

Opting for total commitment, the players (singer Jason Rockman, guitarist Kevin Jardine, bassist Frank Salvaggio and drummer Rob Urbani) upped sticks in 1999 and moved to Los Angeles to be accessible for the city's ever-vigilant A&R people, quickly securing support slots with Motörhead, Papa Roach and System Of A Down after the release of another demo, *Klepto*.

The big break came when Sharon and Ozzy Osbourne were passed a copy of the tape, saw the band perform a brief showcase and asked them to sign to their own Divine Recordings label. Pen and paper duly met and SOD were booked to perform on the 2000 Ozzfest.

An album, *Inches From The Mainline*, was recorded with Iggy Pop/Black Sabbath producer Thom Panunzio and issued on the Slaves' return from the Ozzfest.

SLIPKNOT

www.slipknot1.com
www.peopleequalsshit.com

Unlike many hotly-contested discussions that arise from the mad world of rock, there is no debate about which band is the most intense nu-metal act on the planet at the time of writing. This band is Slipknot. And be warned: they are like no other group ever formed.

Turn to any interview with this nine-man outfit and you'll find plenty of intelligence and good humour, but your overwhelming impression will be one of anger. Presented with a Slipknot song, any psychologist worth his salt wouldn't hesitate to pin down this rage as a reaction to the sterility of the environment in which they grew up - the city of Des Moines, state capital of Iowa in America's Midwest and best is described as Averageville.

SLIPKNOT: Corey Taylor tripping the live fantastic

After many personnel changes, Slipknot's line-up has stabilised as Corey Taylor (vocals), Mick Thompson (guitar), James Root (guitar), Paul Gray (bass), Joey Jordison (drums), Sid Wilson (DJ), Craig Jones (samples), Chris Fehn (percussion) and Shawn Crahan (percussion). The members initially assigned themselves numbers, wishing to avoid being identified by their names and faces - an early attempt to subvert the music scene's cult of personality, an issue which they semi-successfully continue to confront.

Shawn Crahan was the original founder of the band, together with fellow drummer Anders Colsefni. Both had honed their percussive skills in high-school bands Heads On The Wall and Vexx, and Colsefni had also developed a deep, aggressive vocal style. Having become friends in 1994 through attending each other's gigs - and the fact that they both looked like nutters, with mohican haircuts and a clutch of grim tattoos - the two would meet in Crahan's parents' house and play a *Dungeons & Dragons*-style role-playing game called *Rage*. This identity-swapping game was the root of Slipknot's later masked approach.

After several months of abortive attempts to form a band, a tentative line-up formed with Anders' friend Donnie Steele on guitar and Paul Gray on bass (both had been in a death metal band with Anders named Body Pit). The band would jam either in Crahan's parents' garage or in Colsefni's basement and, with the addition of second guitarist Josh Brainard of the local band Modifidious, a full sound began to emerge. The band debated playing gigs, but nothing was booked for two reasons. Firstly, by this stage - mid-1995 - they didn't feel ready to play live, and secondly, Des Moines was notoriously short of decent venues. And remember, this was the American Midwest - you can't just drive over to the next town. The nearest big city to Des Moines is Chicago, 300 miles east.

However, with the recruitment of the prodigiously talented drummer Joey Jordison, the still-unchristened band felt closer to gig-readiness. Ultimately the issue was decided for them when a local promoter needed a band for a forthcoming charity concert at a club called the Crowbar; the band duly performed a set in November 1995 under the name Meld, which Josh had suggested as appropriate given their willingness to experiment with a variety of musical styles.

Despite the relatively warm reception the band received at the Crowbar, all was not well: Donnie suddenly stopped coming to practice. It emerged later that he had experienced some form of religious revelation and felt that being a member of the band was in conflict with his new-found Christianity. His replacement was the teenage Craig Jones, a self-confessed rave kid who knew little about the old-school hip-hop influences that Colsefni was trying to bring to the band. The name Meld was deemed too 'ugly' (Josh had also been humiliated to discover that a meld is a poker move) and the band's new name was taken from 'Slipknot', one of their songs. It went on to become the opening song at a series of gigs which took place at another venue, the Safari Club.

Jones played only one gig as a guitarist before it was decided that Slipknot would benefit from some samples as part of their sound: a technical expert, Jones (nicknamed '133 MHz' because of the speed of his computer - the state of the art back then) moved to electronic sounds: to this day, one of the most eye-opening aspects of the Slipknot experience are the unusual snatches of music, speech or raw noise which he drops into the songs at unexpected moments. As his replacement on guitar, Colsefni and Crahan then drafted in Mick Thompson from Body Pit, whose main influences were The Beatles and Morbid Angel and who gave lessons at a local guitar store, Ye Olde Guitar Shoppe.

After Mick's arrival, things started to move more rapidly for Slipknot. They became friends with Sophia John, a program director at the local radio station KKDM, who had record industry contacts and who agreed to manage them free of charge for a year. Her station then hosted a local Battle Of The Bands, which Slipknot won (no nepotism implied!) defeating their main Des Moines rivals in the process, an alternative rock band called Stone Sour (named after a cocktail), which featured Corey Taylor on vocals.

At around this time, the band arrived for rehearsal one evening to find that Shawn Crahan had brought along a clown mask. Initially he merely hung it on the front of his kit, but later tried it on for the session. Wearing it for the rehearsal allowed him to act as strangely as he wanted, he claimed; he had dug it out of his basement

one day and had thought it might come in useful. Up to this point, Slipknot hadn't really experimented with unusual accessories, on or off stage; Joey - rapidly becoming one of the band's more vocal members - was taken with the idea and soon the other members were wearing their own masks for gigs. When interviewed by

most exciting band I've seen for years." The combination of technical accuracy, layered complexity and sheer venom that made up the Slipknot approach convinced McMahon to sign a production contract with the band, and Slipknot booked into the studio in December to begin recording their first album.

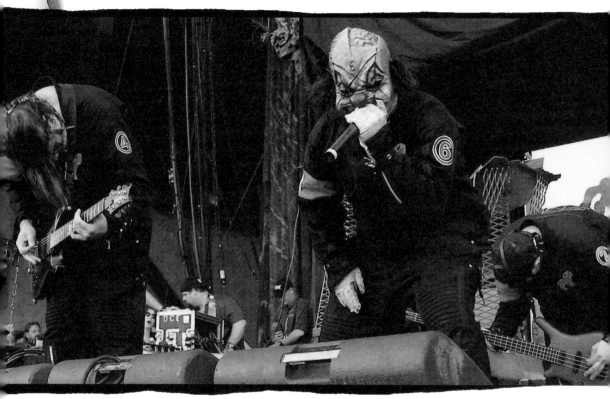

SLIPKNOT: Stand well clear!

the press, they said that the masks allowed their inner personalities to come out, and that the masks revealed more about the wearers than they concealed. Whether or not this was true, the effect on the already frenzied Slipknot shows was galvanic: the band would slam as hard as they possibly could onstage, often damaging their equipment and themselves. The live chaos went so far that Crahan ordered an unbreakable titanium drum kit that could survive the repeated onslaughts.

In late 1995, the band visited a local recording studio, SR Audio, who then sent a producer, Sean McMahon, to Colsefni's house to watch the band rehearse. SR Audio owner Mike Lawyer later said: "Sean was absolutely blown away. He came in the next morning saying, last night I saw the

The result, *Mate. Feed. Kill. Repeat*, has gone down in metal myth as a landmark recording. Recording the eight tracks in a mere three days - but taking three months to do the mix-down - Slipknot produced an astonishing blend of funk, jazz, death metal and even disco, which confuses and entrances metal fans to this day. If you can get hold of one, that is; only 1,000 copies were pressed under the name of the Ismist distributor, most of which were sent out by McMahon, John and the band as promotional items. The sleeve is a shot of a pain-inducing sculpture created by Shawn and Anders, a mighty beast made from iron girders which was designed to cut into human flesh whenever an attempt was made to move it. A successful launch party on Halloween night in 1996, which attracted metal fans from far and wide, proved that the Midwestern public were prepared to buy into the chaotic Slipknot recipe.

Things were getting serious: the band had invested around $16,000 in the making of *MFKR*, and Slipknot had adopted the masks-and-overalls look as their own. A&R men started to appear, notably from Epic and Roadrunner: however, the consensus was that Slipknot weren't ready to sign, although the local and regional buzz around the band was increasing rapidly.

One day in the summer of 1997, Anders arrived at practice to be told by Crahan that the Stone Sour vocalist Corey Taylor was to be recruited as a second singer. Taylor's mid-range style, it was thought, would complement Colsefni's guttural rumble. He was surprised, but accepted the decision as the best option for the band – but was later told that, in fact, Taylor would be the lead singer, while Anders would play percussion and sing backing vocals. Slipknot continued with this revised line-up for a couple of gigs, but Colsefni eventually decided to quit and did so by announcing his departure at the end of a concert. "I hadn't told them beforehand," he said. "I just announced that I wouldn't be playing with Slipknot any longer." He has since gone on to form Painface.

Colsefni left just as the band received their greatest stroke of luck to date. Sophia John managed to track down producer Ross Robinson, who then came to a rehearsal and, like Sean McMahon before him, was deeply impressed. "They were all on their porch as I was driving up - in the freezing cold, with snow on the ground," he later recalled. "It was ugly outside, this was the winter before I recorded the album... they were waiting for me to drive up and when they saw me they ran inside the house. It was funny." He offered to sign the band through his I Am label, and a deal was struck with Roadrunner, who offered Slipknot a seven-album deal worth $500,000. Not bad for a band who had spent the last three years practising in a basement.

The *Slipknot* album was recorded in 1998 and issued on 29th June 1999, going gold in two weeks and platinum inside three months in the US. A brutally powerful but intelligent record, it has become one of the essential albums of the nu-metal movement, along with Korn's self-titled debut. Josh was replaced by James

Root at this time, leaving the band for reasons which he has never disclosed.

Slipknot's stage act has also turned a few heads. Corey has been known to inhale deeply from a jar containing the corpse of a decaying crow, vomit into a plastic container and empty it into the crowd - who then attempt to drink it. At one Halloween show in Des Moines, the band set up huge movie screens displaying scenes from snuff films, while the band also take a goat's heart on tour with them, 'for luck'. The singer also offers the crowd to inhale through a gas mask plugged into his rectum: they do it, too. Shawn and Chris have also made a practice of urinating on each other during the act, although this ceased abruptly after a show where the liquid came perilously close to a powerful stage light – not a particularly pleasant way to depart this life, you can safely presume.

Stage antics such as these and various tabloid-scaring escapades occupied the best part of 2000 before the band entered the studio in January 2001, once again with Robinson in tow. The band (and Joey in particular) had long been promising that the second album would be several times heavier than the first, itself a monstrously powerful album: sceptics were unconvinced until the release via the Roadrunner website of 'The Heretic Anthem', a beast of a song that momentarily silenced the doubters. When the album itself – tellingly entitled *Iowa* – was released in late July 2001, it was immediately apparent that Jordison had not been exaggerating: a fearsomely heavy collection, it pushed the boundaries of nu-metal to more extreme limits than ever before, with songs like 'People=Shit' (a long-time Knot slogan) containing plenty of pure death metal elements.

Iowa went straight to the top of the UK and US album charts and propelled Slipknot to the forefront of the nu-metal scene. More chart-oriented bands such as Limp Bizkit continue to sell more records than Slipknot, by virtue of their more listenable nature, but the Knot fanbase is one of the most loyal anywhere and a whole subculture of 'maggots' (Slipknot's affectionate label for their fans, who they claim feed off the band) has developed. The band is slated to appear in a remake of the classic *Rollerball* movie, performing 'Left Behind', and the various members have side projects in progress – Shawn and

Corey with solo albums, Joey with his glam-punk band the Rejects, Sid with his DJ Starscream alias and Mick with an as yet-untitled death metal project. Corey also appeared on the second Soulfly album, *Primitive*, and a tribute album to the late Snot singer Lynn Strait called *Strait Up*.

Jordison has stated that Slipknot is too intense an entity to survive more than three or four albums without becoming a self-parody, and this makes sense. But there is no stopping the cult of Slipknot, with or without the band-members themselves: it may be that like The Sex Pistols, The Smiths and Nirvana before them, what Slipknot have started is bigger than the band itself.

Released in 1999, the band's first two singles, 'Vulcan' and the *Smells Like Teen Punk Meat* EP, received rave reviews in the press. Touring with Queens Of The Stone Age in the UK brought them to a wider audience and Torres subsequently became a model for the Urban Decay cosmetics company.

A debut album, *Sonic Jihad*, was released in summer 2001 on the Morpheus label and contained covers of The Beatles' 'She Said She Said' and of The Smiths' 'How Soon Is Now'. Of the latter, ex-Smiths frontman Morrissey said in *Mojo* magazine, "It's a better version than ours". It can be assumed that the lanky Mancunian's tongue was firmly in cheek at the time.

SNOT: Much missed and much copied

SNAKE RIVER CONSPIRACY

www.snakeriverconspiracy.com

An industrial rock band, Snake River Conspiracy is a collaboration between ex-Third Eye Blind frontman Jason Slater and the gothette singer Tobey Torres. Slater stated that he had started the band because "music in general had gotten really stale, so I found Tobey who is the exact opposite of everything I hate about chick rock".

SNOT

Having named their band as a joke, the members of Snot were surprised when record companies took them seriously and offered them deals. However, their proficient combination of punk and metal was obviously just what the industry had been looking for: it's a sick irony that this band might well have become the next Amen, had tragedy not intervened.

In spring 1995, surrounded by grim-faced Californian rock bands, guitarist Mike Doling decided to put together a band for fun purposes only, and started looking for like-minded musicians. Recruiting singer Lynn Strait (a New York State-born punk fan who had immersed himself in the Californian scene), guitarist Sonny Mayo, bassist John 'Tumor' Fahnestock and drummer Larkin (from May 1996, Jamie 'Alien' Miller), the band gelled almost immediately and a more adept, hard-hitting sound than any of the players had expected was produced.

Just one year after Snot had formed, they were signed by Geffen, perhaps due to the fact that each man had learned his chops in the old school – Doling had honed his skills in the West Coast speed metal band Kronix and Strait had played bass for the punk outfit Lethal Dose, while the other three had all played with the hardcore band MF Pit Bulls.

Renowned producer Garth Richardson heard the Snot demo and liked it, but the first album, *Get Some*, was ultimately produced by sometime House Of Pain and Helmet console-meister T-Ray in late 1996, and issued shortly afterwards. When journalists asked why some of the lyrics seemed so lightweight, Strait responded with a sneer: "All these LA bands have causes... If we have a message, it's to not take yourself too seriously. All we are is politically incorrect. We like eatin' steaks."

But successful as *Get Some* was, it was destined to be the only Snot recording. Tragically, Strait was killed in a car accident in December, 2000: both band and industry were profoundly shocked. Messages of goodwill came in from many well-known figures in the punk and metal scenes, and Doling decided to attempt a tribute album. Finding people to appear on it was the easy part: the question was which music to include. Eventually, the remaining members of Snot recorded the music to songs that they had written with Lynn and asked various friends to contribute lyrics and vocals.

The result, *Strait Up*, was an impressive collection: guests included Corey Taylor, Max Cavalera, Jonathan Davis, Serj Tankian of System Of A Down and a host of others. The album was released in late 2000 and became a finely-crafted epitaph to the Snot story. Doling joined Soulfly: Fahnestock and Mayo rejoined their old bandmate Larkin in Amen.

SNUB

www.snub.co.uk

For six years Snub knocked out a refreshing blend of hardcore and metal, with a solid fanbase despite the constantly-fluctuating line-up. Formed in March 1995, the final group consisted of Choff (vocals), Oz (guitar), Simon (guitar), Martin (bass) and Vin (drums). The band recorded three demos, which persuaded the Copro label to offer them a deal. An EP, *360 Degree Conviction*, appeared in 1998 and tours with Misery Loves Co and Earthtone9 followed. A full-length album, *Memories In Richter*, brought more fans to the altar of Snub, and the tour wheels started turning again, with the band supporting acts such as One Minute Silence, Stampin' Ground, Medulla Nocte, Napalm Death, Kill II This and the Misfits. In March 2001, the band-members temporarily lost faith in the ability of the industry to project UK bands beyond underground status and Snub split. However, they soon regrouped with renewed vigour and are poised to embark on a live and recording schedule at the time of writing.

SNUB: Now you see 'em, now you don't

SOULFLY

www.soulflytribe.com

Imagine a debate over 'The Top 10 Figures In Nu-Metal'. If you took the scene as a whole entity, the answers (after plenty of heated debate, of course) would probably look something like this.

Ross Robinson is the most influential producer. Shawn Crahan is the most driven performer. Jonathan Davis is the most tortured writer. Roadrunner is the most pioneering label. Fred Durst is the most cunning at marketing an image. And on you'd go, until you came to the most important category: the most influential musician in nu-metal. Various names would be suggested and discarded, as it's no easy choice – after all, there are several equally important bands to consider, even outside the obvious Big Three, including Marilyn Manson, Deftones, Fear Factory, Amen and Nine Inch Nails. But the answer I'd go for (feel free to let me know if you disagree: you'll find my e-mail address in the introduction) would be Max Cavalera, sometime of Sepultura and now of Soulfly. The nature of his pioneering status can be assessed only by studying the career of this remarkable musician, whose political agenda makes him more than just a cultural figure – to his fans, he's practically an icon.

Part of the appeal that Cavalera has for his fans lies in the fact that he comes from humble beginnings. Unlike his baseball-capped white-bread contemporaries, he was born and grew up in Belo Horizonte in Brazil, the country's third largest conurbation and a true Third World city if ever there was one. Developing a passion for heavy metal at a young age, he began playing guitar in a teenage band in the early Eighties, influenced strongly by the aggressive sounds coming from Britain and the brand-new Californian extreme metal scene: in fact, the first three albums he ever bought (on his first trip to Sao Paulo) were records by Iron Maiden, Metallica and Slayer. As Brazil had only recently emerged from the grip of the military dictatorship which had held sway for the previous two decades, gaining access to underground music such as metal and punk was difficult – and therefore, all the more desirable for the typical rebellious teenager.

Naming his band Sepultura ('sepulchre' or 'grave' in Portuguese), Max recruited his drummer brother Igor, a second guitarist, Jairo T, and a bass player, Paulo Jr. (who would later revert to his full name of Paulo Pinto). The band's early work was focused purely on speed, for the simple reason that at the time there were only three types of heavy metal – traditional mid-tempo classic metal (Maiden, Motörhead, Black Sabbath), blow-waved commercial nonsense (Warrant, Poison, Ratt) and the fiercely speedy sound of thrash. The last version of the genre made most sense in the uncompromising world of Sepultura, and so the early recordings were all about velocity, with the secondary focus on the topics of war, social decay and Satanism (the preferred topics of almost every youthful old-metal band).

Persuading the tiny local Cogumelo label to offer them a deal in 1985, the band recorded four laughably primitive tracks for a split LP with another Brazilian band, the now-vanished Overdose. Their sound was tinny and murky at the same time, with Cavalera's schoolboy lyrics barked incomprehensibly over the warp-speed riffs, although the fact that any of it was audible at all is commendable, given Sepultura's almost complete lack of resources and expertise.

The album, *Bestial Devastation*, sank without trace. However, Cogumelo were willing to fund a full-length recording, and sessions commenced for the *Morbid Visions* album. Although this contained more of the same – amateurish lyrics and songwriting and a dismally poor production – it did spawn a hit, the very Slayer-influenced 'Troops Of Doom'. One or two journalists began to take Sepultura seriously and, inspired by this, the band moved to Sao Paulo to try to build a local following. This decision, plus the replacement of Jairo T with the more adept Andreas Kisser, led to a giant step forward in quality between *Morbid Visions* and the next album, *Schizophrenia*, the band's final Cogumelo release. Like Metallica before them – whose hamfisted debut, *Kill 'Em All*, bore little resemblance to its polished successor, *Ride The Lightning* – Sepultura were suddenly perceived as a force to be reckoned with, and international attention began to focus on this band from this most unlikely of geographical locations.

As with so many other bands in this book, it was the Roadrunner label which secured the Sepultura contract, and the company wasted no time in reissuing *Schizophrenia* worldwide to genuine acclaim. Now honing their sound into a deeper, more brutal death metal approach, Sepultura requested the services of the now-renowned (but then-rookie) producer Scott Burns to work on their third full album, flying him to Rio de Janeiro with amusing consequences (the inexperienced

Burns had items stolen from his hotel room and found the underworld atmosphere of Rio something of a culture shock). The result, 1989's *Beneath The Remains*, caused a sensation and has gone down in extreme metal history as one of the finest thrash metal albums ever made.

At this stage there were signs that Max was outgrowing his somewhat juvenile obsession with speed for its own sake, and the song sections which weren't dedicated to blinding velocity were becoming more inventive. Tours with Sodom in Europe saw more audiences converted to the Sepultura cause (punk fans in particular responded to Max's stripped-down playing – he famously

Chaos AD abandoned speed metal entirely, except for the classic 'Biotech Is Godzilla', an anti-corporate, pro-ecology rant penned by the Dead Kennedys' Jello Biafra. After touring the album, Sepultura surprised many observers by retreating into silence for some time. Finally, the next album to appear was their most experimental yet: emphasising mostly Latin American-focused issues such as social deprivation and tribal exploitation, *Roots* (1996) saw Cavalera recruit Ross Robinson to produce and the band daub themselves in tribal paint for the artwork. Robinson's involvement caused a few sneers among the extreme metal cognoscenti, who complained that the

SOULFLY: Uncompromisingly heavy

uses only four strings on his guitars, never feeling the need to improve his self-confessedly rudimentary lead guitar skills), but only one further genuine thrash metal album remained: 1991's *Arise*. Perhaps due to the record's more balanced combination of heaviness with speed, it went platinum, and Sepultura took it on a world tour.

Cavalera's subsequent actions were all similarly against the grain. Firstly, he married Sepultura manager Gloria Bujnowski, an older partner than is usual for a person in their early twenties. He then wrote material for a new album that was more hardcore punk than metal: 1993's

producer had been chosen only because of the enormous success of Korn's recent debut album, and – worse – that Cavalera had wanted Ross simply to help him copy the fat sound of the Korn record on *Roots*. The sonic profile of both albums is certainly similar, and Korn themselves were rumoured to be unhappy at this development.

However, Max sailed through this with confidence intact – a man who has learned to live in the Belo Horizonte ghetto doesn't panic at a few disgruntled journalists – and even indulged in a popular side-project, Nailbomb, which featured the talents of Fudge Tunnel's Alex Newport and

Fear Factory's Dino Cazares. A Sepultura compilation, *Blood-Rooted*, also did well. But trouble was coming, and in fact the beginning of the end of the 'old' Sepultura can be attributed to the death in 1996 of Max's adopted stepson Dana Wells, who had been murdered by still-unidentified killers. The announcement came on the same day that Sepultura were due to perform at the UK's Monsters Of Rock festival: headliner Ozzy Osbourne lent the Cavaleras his private jet to take them back to Brazil. The gig went ahead, with Kisser standing in on vocals.

The band regrouped after some time off, but Cavalera was still deeply in mourning. Matters weren't helped when the other three members of the band approached him in late 1996 to express their dissatisfaction at Gloria's involvement with Sepultura and asked him to consider finding another manager. An enormous row blew up and Max left the band in fury. At the time of writing, the two bands are still not reconciled, despite the fact that one of Sepultura's members is none other than Max's brother Igor. Kisser, Pinto and Cavalera Jr. struggled without Max for a time, and it was even thought that a cessation of activities might be on the cards: however, after considering making Andreas the permanent vocalist, a frontman was recruited – ex-Outface singer Derrick Greene – and the 'new' Sepultura have gone on to release two moderately successful albums, *Against* (1999) and *Nation* (2001), although the recent news that they and Roadrunner have parted ways has been a disappointment for their many loyal fans.

But it is Max, of course, who plays the bigger part – in this book at least. Almost broken by the death of Wells and the split of the band with which he had played for ten full years, Cavalera was plagued by depression and needed some form of musical activity to help him get back on his feet. Forming a band with sometime Sepultura bass roadie Marcello D. Rapp, ex-Chico Science guitarist Jackson Bandeira and ex-Thorn drummer Roy 'Rata' Mayorga, Cavalera christened his new band Soulfly (appropriate, given the life-and-death issues he was struggling with at the time) and played some low-key gigs. Much of the Sepultura fanbase turned out to witness his new material – a heavier, darker, and above all *angrier* combination of riffing and roaring than ever before – and a deal was soon inked with Roadrunner. Sessions for an album commenced in late 1997.

The first record, a self-titled effort released early the following year and featuring homages to Wells and a satisfyingly rich tapestry of musical styles, was received with acclaim by fans and press – so much so that Roadrunner reissued it in 1999 with remixes and live tracks, including a song recorded as Brazil's World Cup soccer anthem for the championship held the same year. The great and the good of nu-metal had queued up to appear on the album, including Fred Durst and DJ Lethal from Limp Bizkit, Burton C. Bell, Dino Cazares and Christian Olde Wolbers of Fear Factory, Chino Moreno of the Deftones, Benji from Dub War and Eric Bobo from Cypress Hill.

The result was a visceral, anguished album – Ross Robinson had produced it and in trademark style (see Slipknot, Korn and Glassjaw) had induced Cavalera to enunciate every shred of agony in him. And so Max's journey from the pinnacle of old thrash metal (*Beneath The Remains*, released just nine years earlier) to a position in which members of the press were labelling him 'the godfather of nu-metal' was complete. No-one was more bemused at this than Cavalera himself, who profoundly dislikes the categorisation that has always dogged his music.

Tours with Rammstein and the Ozzfest ensued and, within a short time, it seemed that the metal public had gravitated to Soulfly. Max began making appearances at music industry events (the New Music Marathon in New York and Holland's Crossing Boarder Festival of 1997, for example) and guesting on other rock acts' albums – Deftones' *Around The Fur* featured a notable cameo. Many thought his agreement to sing a theme for Sprite in his home country was a strange move, however, although he explained it as an act of punk insurrection from within the corporate enemy. And few dared to disagree...

After more tours, the recruitment of a new drummer, Joe Nunez, and the replacement of Jackson with Logan Mader – whose place was in turn taken by ex-Snot six-stringer Mikey Doling – Soulfly began recording a second album. This turned out to be a more considered and less cathartic record: Cavalera had recently become a Christian and was evidently in more relaxed

SPIKESHANK: Rather like a younger, prettier Fear Factory

– if no less hungry – frame of mind. Released in late 2000, *Primitive* contained several songs which had more in common with world music and soul than the enormo-metal of before, although the album's core was pure riffing, with 'Jumpdafuckup' (featuring Slipknot's Corey Taylor) and 'Terrorist' (with Slayer's Tom Araya) definite high points. It seems that Max was more contented with the new line-up (he said: "The rock star shit does not work for us. Some people came into this band and didn't understand that"), and was happier to explore feelings other than pure anger. For instance, his collaboration with Sean Lennon, 'Son Song', was a paean to the sadness both men felt at growing up without a father.

Cavalera's current prominence in music is underlined by the fact that many members of the press have started calling him 'the Bob Marley of metal'. Although he shrugs this term off in some embarrassment, there are certain obvious parallels between him and Jamaica's most famous export: both men came from the Third World, rising above poverty and urban squalor in the process; both sought to spread a political message in their music, and have transcended the limits of their music in doing so; and both will be remembered as men of courage and vision.

So, the most influential musician in nu-metal, then. Still think it's Fred Durst? Think again.

SPINESHANK

www.spineshank.com

Hailed by many critics at the time of writing as the Nu-Metal Band Most Likely To Succeed, on the basis of a finely-crafted second album, some gripping hit singles and a knack with a melodic hook, the LA quartet Spineshank first formed in early 1996 from the ashes of a band called Basic Enigma, which – according to popular legend – decided to call it a day when they heard Fear Factory's *Demanufacture*.

Made up of the usefully-cheekboned singer Johnny Santos, guitarist Mike Sarkisyan, bassist Robert Garcia and drummer Tom Decker, Spineshank have occasionally been sniped at for the resemblance of their sound to the electronic fizz of the Factory – whose guitarist Dino Cazares offered them a support slot at the Whiskey A-Go-Go – but appear to have risen above this by virtue of the simple high quality of their material, which is poppy enough for the kiddies but heavy enough for the die-hards.

Opening gigs for bands of the calibre of Sepultura, Snot, Coal Chamber and Danzig brought Spineshank to the attention of – guess who? – Roadrunner in 1997, and a debut album, *Strictly Diesel*, was released the following year. Fear Factory vocalist Burton C. Bell featured on the song 'Stain' and the album was a moderate success, but it was 2000's *Height Of Callousness* which really propelled Spineshank to the big time, with its meaty production courtesy of Gggarth and a clutch of almost annoyingly catchy songs, including the MTV hit 'New Disease'. They remain almost certain to reap further rewards.

SPITE

From the small-town background of Charlotte, North Carolina, Spite is made up of vocalist Chris Boone, guitarist Craig Baker, bassist Josh Pratt and drummer Byron McDonald and was first mooted as a band in the summer of 1996. Metal was different back then: Korn reigned supreme (and still sounded fairly new), and the harsh sounds of death metal which fellow hicksville-dwellers such as Slipknot would later bring to the arena of nu-metal were still very much the province of the underground.

However, Spite soon developed a sparse, economical (but still blindingly heavy) brand of metal and took it on tour, travelling up and down the East Coast seemingly ad infinitum with a variety of bands. The album *Heavy Whipping Cream* was recorded in 1997 and received a low-key response, possibly due to its self-consciously quirky title (well, it's hardly *Reign In Blood*, is it?), but the band began to attract a following and the Prosthetic label

approached them with the offer of a deal.

The next album, the nationally-distributed *Bastard Complex*, was released in 1999, and although it was hailed as a deft piece of work by various members of the press, Spite have so far failed to capitalise on its success and remain in the lower echelons of nu-metal.

STAIND

www.staind.com

As Korn were responsible for Limp Bizkit, so the Bizkit are responsible for Staind: this is a common procedure in the world of modern metal, where bands agree to help each other out if one of them makes it to the big time. It's either a selfless act or a selfish one, depending on your point of view, but either way it's been the cause of many a hit single and lucrative support slot in recent years.

The New England band Staind were formed in 1994 by vocalist/guitarist Aaron Lewis, guitarist Mike Mushok and drummer Jon Wysocki. Like many of the bands here, they had to pay their dues before fame came knocking, and three long years of touring in the area helped them sell 2,000 copies of a self-released debut album, *Tormented*. Bands that shared a stage

STAIND: Nu-metal's first superstars

with them were many and various, including relatively big names like Gwar and lesser-knowns such as Honkeyball, Far and God Lives Under Water.

At one point it seemed that Staind would tread the provincial boards forever, but a lucky break came in the form of Limp Bizkit, whose show one evening in Hartford, Connecticut, the band were scheduled to open. First meetings with the soon-to-be-biggest nu-metal band in the world were inauspicious: Staind had been selling their album at the venue and Bizkit singer Fred Durst had been handed a copy. Reacting negatively to the slightly demonic cover art of the CD, Durst demanded to

demo tracks. Unable to contact Durst, whose band had embarked on a protracted touring schedule, Mushok drove directly to the Bizkit's show supporting Deftones in October 1997, parked outside the venue and knocked on the Limp Bizkit tour bus, demo tapes in hand. The door was answered by Bizkit decksman DJ Lethal, who agreed to pass the recordings onto Durst, who was otherwise engaged. The Staind guitarist then watched the concert, but was unable to find Durst afterwards and went home with a sinking feeling.

However, in the early hours of the morning, Mushok's phone rang: it was Fred, who had listened to the tapes, liked what

STAIND: A laundrette joke would be too obvious...

know if Staind were Satanists and apparently refused to believe their denials. Throwing the disc on the table, Durst stalked out and allegedly attempted to have the band removed from the bill.

Forty-five minutes later Durst returned, after Staind had played their set. The members of Staind expected more arguments and were pleasantly surprised when Fred complimented them on their performance, saying that they were the best band he had seen in two years. He also promised to contact them about a production company he was founding and the two parties exchanged phone numbers.

Months passed with no further negotiations and Staind recorded some

he heard and wanted Staind to come to his home town of Jacksonville in Florida, stay at his house, support the Bizkit at a local show and work on some songs. The trip was duly made (hindered only slightly by the breakdown of Staind's bus just before the Florida state line, necessitating a humiliating ride by tow-truck to the Durst residence) and work began immediately on fine-tuning some Staind compositions.

After the concert was successfully completed and four songs had been retweaked, Durst – who had an itinerant role as A&R man for Limp Bizkit's record label, Flip – arranged a meeting between the Flip CEO and Staind. This duly took place in Los Angeles, where a three-track demo was recorded. Durst and DJ Lethal produced the songs and in February 1998 a deal was signed with Flip. More shows followed, this time with Sevendust and Clutch as well as their Limp labelmates, after which all parties returned to Florida for more studio sessions.

Veteran producer Terry Date was called in to produce a debut album, *Dysfunction*, which was recorded after Staind appeared on the Vans Warped tour. Released in April 1999, it was a slow burner, picking up significant sales only after several shows had taken place, but a niche was slowly being carved out for Staind, helped along by support slots in 2000 with Kid Rock and yes, Limp Bizkit.

Truly, nu-metal moves in mysterious ways. Whatever next? Alien Ant Farm entering the charts with a Michael Jackson cover? Oh – hold on a minute...

STAMPIN' GROUND

www.stampin-ground.com

As we've seen many times in this book, the essence of nu-metal is its variety, and its willingness to accept all kinds of music into itself. For example, if it's gothic gloom you're after, look no further than Coal Chamber, Marilyn Manson or Misery Loves Company. If hip-hop is your thing, you can

STAMPIN' GROUND: The ultimate live experience?

The month before this book was completed, everything was turned on its head for Staind as their second proper album, *Break The Cycle*, outdid both their rappin' mentors and every other nu-metal band on the horizon by hitting the top spot in both American and UK album charts. A buzz had been building about Staind in previous months, due to the success of two singles: the first, 'Outside' was unique in that it had been performed exactly once (at a festival with Durst on vocals), recorded and issued to enormous airplay. The second, 'It's Been Awhile' was a more straightforward MTV-assisted hit, with its memorable video of a performance in a gloomy, candle-lit studio.

mix it up with Korn and Limp Bizkit. A taste of death metal can be had courtesy of Slipknot. And if it's punk you're after, there are two bands in this book that you must see before you die. One of them is Amen. And the other one is Stampin' Ground.

While Amen represent the glamorous, LA-and-leather side of punk-metal, with their undeniably handsome singer Casey Chaos, Stampin' Ground are decidedly down to earth. Spawned by the UK hardcore scene, but far too enamoured of classic thrash and death metal to let the old metallic sound die off completely, the quintet produces a sound almost unparalleled in its fury, which appeals to punks, metallers and even classic rock fans.

The band were first formed in early 1995 in the south-west of England, with the somewhat bizarre aim of playing slow hardcore punk. This proved to be as dull as it sounds, and it was only a matter of days before the superfast likes of Slayer proved to be the most powerful influence on the new band. Stampin' Ground moved quickly, recording demos in early and mid-1995, both of which attracted record company attention and led to deals being offered. However, true to the spirit of their punk backgrounds, the band members decided to put in some solid touring time before selecting a record label, and in any case personnel changes (the drummer was replaced and the singer, Paul, returned to his main band, the well-known Medulla Nocte) made the future slightly difficult to predict. This left the line-up as Heath (vocals), Mobs (guitar), Scott (guitar), Ian (bass) and Ade (drums), who consolidated their skills by recording more tracks.

Live shows followed, with the flourishing hardcore scene providing plenty of support opportunities: opening shows for the likes of Unborn, Above All and Withdrawn honed the SG live skills significantly, and the band were soon asked to perform on bills with bigger names such as Sick Of It All. At this time a 7" single, 'Dawn Of Night', was released on the Days Of Fury label, swiftly followed by another, 'Starved', which was issued by the New York label Too Damn Hype. After a European tour, Stampin' Ground began to find themselves regular fixtures on all-day punk festivals with bands such as Knuckledust, Freebase and Outbreak, as well as old-school punks The Exploited and even the death metal stalwarts Napalm Death: proof of their acceptability on a variety of scenes.

A German label, We Bite, reissued the first two singles on one CD EP in late 1996, marking the end of two busy years in the world of Stampin' Ground. A full-length album, the very Deicide-titled *Demons Run Amok*, was recorded in early 1997 and released by We Bite in April, while more SG tunes found their way onto a Too Damn Hype 7" and a compilation from the well-respected Household Name label.

European shows upped the ante once more: performances with established bands such as the Misfits, Agnostic Front and Earth Crisis brought the Ground to a whole new audience, although the progress of the band was halted somewhat when relations between Heath and the other band-members became strained and he was obliged to leave. In a twist of fate, this meant pulling out of scheduled shows with the legendary Canadian progressive thrashers Voivid. However, in early 1998 a replacement – Adam from Blood Oath – was signed up and shows were lined up. Good news came when the major metal label Century Media approached Stampin' Ground with an offer of a deal, which the band were pleased to accept, having lost some confidence in the abilities of We Bite.

After yet more European dates – this time on the same bills as metal behemoths such as Slayer and Suicidal Tendencies – a second album, *An Expression Of Repressed Violence*, was recorded. The underground and mainstream metal press applauded its convincing ferocity, and the band took it on tour with the old-school New York punks Cause For Alarm.

After a split EP was recorded with Knuckledust and released in 1999 by bassist Ian Glasper on his own Blackfish label (it went on to receive the Single Of The Week accolade in *Kerrang!*, voted there by none other than guest reviewers Monster Magnet), Stampin' Ground played with Freebase and rap-metallers One Minute Silence. In July the band toured the US for the first time, sharing the bill with Cause For Alarm, Leeway, Mushmouth, Blood For Blood and Voice Of Reason, before embarking on the British UKHC Tour, a showcase for some of this country's best underground bands.

All this preparation paid off in 2000, when the band's Century Media debut, *Carved From Empty Words*, made Stampin' Ground into one of the most internationally prominent hardcore bands in any country. A scintillating, vengeful album, *CFEW* received rave reviews in the international media and became the standard frame of reference for many a hardcore album reviewer. But what made the band so popular with their fans was their constant refusal to stop touring the clubs and pubs that made their name, and their determination to remain true to the ideals of the hardcore scene that had nurtured them. There's integrity here, readers, and in the world of popular music, that's a rare quality indeed.

STATIC-X

www.teamstatic-x.com

Few metal bands would dare to apply a label as unusual as 'rhythmic trancecore' to their music, for fear of instant ridicule. But on the other hand, few bands – apart from the hardest-core of punk acts, that is – would be proud to feature a frontman with foot-high vertically-spiked hair, either. Static-X do both.

Corgan of Smashing Pumpkins, an unsigned act at the time, who rehearsed in the same space as Deep Blue Dream.

Big as the Windy City undoubtedly was, the pair realised that California was the place for any new band to be and decided to relocate to Los Angeles. On arrival in their new hometown, they placed an ad for a guitarist – quickly answered by the Japanese six-stringer Koicki Fukada, who is said to have walked into the rehearsal room holding the advert and saying, "I'm your

STATIC-X: Hair today, gone tomorrow?

Originally from the cornfields of America's Midwest, and specifically the towns of Shelby, Michigan (where the aforementioned singer, guitarist and barber's nightmare Wayne Static was born) and Jamaica, Illinois (hometown of drummer Ken Jay), the roots of Static-X began in Chicago, to which the two had gravitated as an escape route from their respective hick-town backgrounds. Wayne formed a gloomy, black-clad goth band called Deep Blue Dream, and Ken worked in a record shop while backing various local metal acts. The two met after being introduced by Ken's co-worker, none other than Billy

new guitarist". With the recruitment of bassist Tony Campos – who had played in several local death metal bands – the line-up was complete and, after songs had been written and honed, a strenuous live schedule began to take shape. Becoming tired of explaining that the S-X sound was supposed to combine rock, metal, techno, goth and industrial sounds into one, the 'rhythmic trancecore' label was devised (it seems that no-one laughed) and label interest began to grow.

A deal was signed with Warners in early 1998 and an album, *Wisconsin Death Trip*, was recorded some months later. Based on a century-old folk tale (and bearing comparison with the following year's foresty *Blair Witch Project* spookfest), the concept behind the album came from a book that Wayne had unearthed in a flea market. The record rapidly went gold and a buzz grew around Static-X, who responded by getting their heads down to some serious touring. This ultimately proved too much for Fukada, whose departure was less arrogant than his arrival. His replacement was ex-Dope axeman Tripp Eisen.

Since then the band has been on the up and up, with MTV buying into the Static image and tours with System of A Down, Fear Factory and Morbid Angel cementing their rise. A *Wisconsin Death Trip* single, 'Bled For Days', was issued by Korn on their *Extra Values* bonus CD and on the *Bride Of Chucky* soundtrack. The follow-up album, *Machine*, was released in August 2001 and was accompanied by major publicity.

Proof of the band's penetration into the unlikeliest of areas came in 1999 when Wayne was involved in a car accident: an ambulance paramedic, trying to keep the injured singer conscious, asked him what his job was and, hearing that his patient fronted Static-X, responded that he was a big fan and had been on the mailing list for some time. He is now on the guest list for life.

SUNLOUNGER

www.sunlounger.co.uk

Hotly tipped to rise to the top of the nu-metal movement before too long, Sunlounger come from the initially uninspiring environs of Barnsley in South Yorkshire and were formed in February 1998. Consisting of Lee Storrar, Chris Potts and Pete Williams, Sunlounger wasted little time before entering a recording studio and an EP, *Mealticket*, appeared that summer. A track from the recording appeared on a Metal Hammer cover CD, *21st Century Media Blitz II*, and various metal journalists began to froth at the mouth about Sunlounger's formidable live presence and songwriting abilities.

A second EP, *Personal Services*, appeared on the band's own Savour At Volume label, before a single, 'Puppy Fat', became Sunlounger's debut for Org. Despite the replacement of drummer Williams with Lee Hardman, the band's future seems rosy – if they can match up to the profile that has been built up for them by the press, that is.

SUNNA

http://melankolic.astralwerks.com/sunna/story.html

A five-man band focused around the guitar, vocal and songwriting abilities of Londoner Jon Harris, Sunna are signed to the Melankolic label, home to the Bristol hip-hop pioneers Massive Attack. Harris was responsible for the murky, wall-of-sound guitars which appeared on the Massive's third album, *Mezzanine*, and which marked a departure for the West Country trio.

A fan of AC/DC, Neil Young and Soundgarden, Harris also incorporates darker influences such as Tool into the Sunna sound, backed up by guitarist Ian MacLaren, bassist Shane Goodwin, ex-Cable drummer Richie Mills and DJ Flatline. His band's name represents 'faith without religion', he explains. The sole Sunna album to date is 2000's *One Minute Science*, a thoughtful, intense record, which prompted Tool frontman Maynard James Keenan to invite them on the road in that year with his successful side project A Perfect Circle. A Sunna song, 'Power Struggle', was also used on the soundtrack of Paul Verhoeven's deeply unremarkable *Invisible Man* remake, *Hollow Man*.

SYSTEMATIC

www.systematic1.com

The East Bay Area quartet Systematic were formed in 1996 and consists of Tim Narducci (vocals/guitar), Adam Ruppel (guitar), Nick St. Denis (bass) and Phillip Bailey (drums – later replaced by Shaun Bannon). Narducci and Ruppel initially produced demo recordings as a duo, bringing influences as disparate as Nine Inch Nails, Alice In Chains, Massive Attack and Led Zeppelin to the sessions, but later recruited St. Denis and Bailey: the former had seen some success as a guitarist in the long-standing hardcore band Pro Pain.

After nailing a sequence of well-received shows in the San Francisco area, Systematic's big break came when a friend, a tape operator at the Plant studio in Sausalito, happened to be playing a Systematic demo CD when Metallica drummer Lars Ulrich was tweaking

SYSTEM OF A DOWN: One of the strangest (and most interesting) bands ever formed

material for his band's *S&M* album of 1999. The Danish headbanger was impressed with what he heard, borrowed the album and offered the band a deal with his Music Company label two weeks later.

Noted producer Peter Collins (Ultraspank, Rush) was roped in to handle Systematic's first album, *Somewhere In Between*, a powerful, innovative record with melody and heaviness in abundance. The studio sessions were followed up by tours with weighty names such as Staind, Godsmack and Nothingface, allowing the band to face a wider public than previously possible and making a step to the next level more plausible. The fact that many fans tend to get understandably confused between Systematic and System Of A Down is a mere fly in the ointment.

SYSTEM OF A DOWN

www.systemofadown.com

To the layman, many bands of a given type sound very similar. In the nu-metal world, there are dozens of bands which produce riffs of more or less heaviness, rap or roar with varying amounts of angst and over which DJs of pretty much one baseball-hatted species make the usual wicky-wicky-wack noises. This is to be expected – it's the way it is, and the way round it is to listen hard for the differences in the music, which are there for anyone to hear.

A good way for a rock band to avoid sounding too much like its peers is to make a deliberate effort to push out the envelope. Often, this means making odd, unorthodox or downright strange music. This can backfire, of course: for every Faith No More or Jane's Addiction (who can make quirky, bizarre sounds without sounding like schoolboys), there's a Twiztid (who can't). It's a question of where to draw the line: sudden tempo changes, unexpected comedy samples and weird style-shifts can be great, or they can be pointless.

One nu-metal band that does sound refreshingly dissimilar to the standard rap-rock template, however, is System Of A Down, an act that draws several styles under its wing and which has gained cult status in a short time on the scene. The four Los Angelenos immediately stand out from the pack due to the simple fact that they come from America's small Armenian community, and bring the melodies of traditional Eastern European songs, as well as an outsider's perspective packed with considerable vitriol, to their music.

The bare bones of their story are interesting, but have much in common with many other bands included here. Serj Tankian (vocals), Daron Malakian (guitar), Shavo Odadjian (bass) and John Dolmayan (drums) had been playing in various LA bands since 1993, but first formed a group together in 1995 in Southern California, producing a much sought-after three-song demo which penetrated the furthest echelons of the tape-trading underground – even showing up in New Zealand and, unsurprisingly, Eastern Europe. Building a live following in Los Angeles, SOAD (named after a poem by Malakian entitled *Victims Of A Down*, although Serj says "Take your own meaning out of our name. It means different things to different people") attracted the attention of veteran metal producer Rick Rubin, who signed them to his American label shortly after it had closed a distribution agreement with Columbia.

Rubin produced System's self-titled debut album and American released it in the summer of 1998. The record rapidly went stratospheric and the band played a fistful of important tours, including jaunts with Slayer and the inevitable Ozzfest. The album was reissued in the summer of 2001 to coincide with the release of *Toxicity*, which was the most eagerly-anticipated metal record of 2001 (apart from Slipknot's *Iowa*) and which hit the top spot on the US album charts shortly after its release.

What is more fascinating than the mere facts of the SOAD biography is the mindset which drives the players. Tankian has said that the band's goal is "to stay open to whatever currents guide us through our lives – in every way, to be ourselves". If System has an agenda, it is based on an anti-racist, anti-capitalist credo, but even this is too simple an explanation for the anger which is portrayed in their music. 'P.L.U.C.K.', for example – meaning Politically Lying, Unholy, Cowardly Killers – has been labelled by the band as "a revolutionary song... to do with the Armenian genocide", while other political themes include the hypocrisy of the military intelligence system and outrage at the activities of covert organisations such as the CIA.

So, a deeply unusual band, then – even among the bands in this book, which has been written expressly as a guide to bands which have extended the boundaries of rock. The sounds System Of A Down make can seem strange (and by any standards, they often *are* strange), which means that they aren't suited to every listener – but they've managed to change the face of nu-metal, and for that we should be thankful.

SERJ TANKIAN: No, he's not mad – but he does a good impression of it

TAPROOT

www.taprootmusic.com

For many pundits the brand-new hope of nu-metal, Taproot have actually been treading the well-worn path towards metallic recognition since late 1997. Combining incisive rapping and vocal melodies with lyrical introspection and the expected heaviness, the band have become known as the rap-metal band's rap-metal band – even in an age when the phrase itself is dying out.

Their story is one of sheer grit. The foursome (vocalist Stephen Richards, guitarist Michael DeWolf, bassist Philip Lipscomb and drummer Jarrod Montague) met at the University of Michigan. Richards and DeWolf had played in various local death metal bands without really achieving a great deal, until they met the other musicians at college. The newly-formed band's first move was to record a three-track demo, which (perhaps influenced a little by Korn and Kid Rock) was entitled *Pimp Ass Sounds*. This was distributed among the small local following which had built up.

Taproot then built on this fanbase by exploiting the power of the internet as a marketing and distribution tool. It's reported that over 30 fansites had been created as a result of the constant shows Taproot played, and it became obvious that an official site would be useful. This was duly launched and quickly built an impressive hit rate.

Further determination to go it alone if necessary was demonstrated in the spring of 1998, when Taproot recorded and manufactured an album, *Something More Than Nothing*. Over 10,000 copies were sold over the ensuing months, with copies burned at the college labs, hand-packaged by Richards and posted to their local fans. This was followed by the *Mentobe* EP (a play on 'meant to be', presumably) which was reissued as *Upon Us* a year later when extra tracks had been recorded.

So far, so local: as had been the case with one or two other bands already mentioned in these pages, the man who – in another life – would have been responsible for Taproot's jump to the next stage was Limp Bizkit's Fred Durst, who was on the point of releasing his first album *Three Dollar Bill, Y'All$* and was looking for new bands to produce. Stephen had sent him a Taproot demo, and the baseball-capped rapper responded by promising to 'do a Staind', i.e. to get them signed and helm a debut album.

However, there's many a slip, so to speak, and the offer that Fred ultimately made to Taproot seemed less attractive than the deals available from other companies and the contract was never signed. Never backward in coming forward, Durst phoned Richards in a rage. The band returned from LA, where they had been performing a showcase for producer Rick Rubin, to find a message on Stephen's answerphone. Allegedly, Fred's words were "Steve. Fred Durst. Hey man, you fucked up. You don't ever bite the hand that feeds in this business, bro." Taproot were both shocked and amused at the virulence in his tone, but signed a deal with the Velvet Hammer/Atlantic partnership and looked forward to the next stage. It is unknown if the bands have ever been reconciled.

Since then Taproot's star has continued to rise. An album, *Gift*, was received with good reviews in summer 2001: it had been produced by Ulrich Wild (Pantera, Powerman 5000, Static-X) and fans loved it for its power and Richards' perceptive lyrics. A gig at the Hollywood Palladium with Anthrax and Henry Rollins led to the beginning of a friendship with Ozzy and Sharon Osbourne: having performed a showcase for the benefit of Ozzy's teenage son Jack (who is instrumental in choosing the bands that appear on his father's travelling festival, the Ozzfest), the band joined Slipknot and Papa Roach on the 2000 'Fest and their profile has continued to grow. Heaven only knows what will happen as and when their paths cross that of old Fred, though.

311

www.311.com

Edging towards the more lightweight end of the nu-metal spectrum, but deserving of attention nonetheless – if for no other reason than that they have served their time

– the fivesome of 311 come from the city of Omaha in Nebraska and met at high school there in the late Eighties.

Nick Hexum and Tim Mahoney played in a school band called the Eds, while Chad Sexton also played in a jazz band with Nick.

Hexum was the group's prime instigator, leaving town for the bright lights of LA to seek his musical fortune at the tender age of 17. Chad and a keyboard player, Ward Bones, soon followed him to California and the trio set up a band called Unity (never mind that it sounds suspiciously like a girl-band).

However, LA was not for Chad, who soon returned to Omaha and joined a band with Jim Watson and P-Nut. The hometown band was soon outperforming Unity, the latter's veneer of Hollywood glamour notwithstanding, and sure enough Nick soon found himself on the bus back home. This proved to be a wise move, however, as the newly-formed quartet landed a local support slot with Fugazi, who were playing an Omaha gig in June 1990.

The following year saw Watson depart, to be replaced by the also-returned Mahoney, while the final member, SA Martinez, was also recruited. This was the line-up which remains to this day, and they wasted no time in recording no fewer than three independent albums and releasing them on their own What Have You label. Together with these records – *Dammit*, *Hydroponic* and *Unity* – and an ever-growing live reputation, the 311 path seemed clear and the band made a collective decision to move to Los Angeles – this time for good.

A deal with the Capricorn label was signed just as the quintet were on the point of total penury, and an album, *Music*, was recorded and released in February 1993. A setback occurred when the 311 van caught fire while the band were driving to a venue: all their equipment, and even their clothes, were lost, and it says much for the devotion of their small fanbase at this stage that they were able to continue touring, with the loan of instruments and money from fans and friends.

Adopting a release-tour-release schedule, 311 recorded *Grassroots* in 1994 and *311* in 1995, both to some approval but few gasps of delight. A single, 'Down', was released in late 1996, and proved to be the record that would break them at last: it reached the top spot on the *Billboard* rock chart, while its successor, 'All Mixed Up', made No. 2.

After releasing the enormo-hit album *Transistor* in 1996 and touring the record in Australia, New Zealand, the UK and Japan, material from 311's first three indie albums was reissued on the *Omaha Session* EP, once more on the What Have You label. A live album, the imaginatively-titled *311 Live*, was released in November 1998 and a year later the band recorded yet another studio album, *Soundsystem*.

Having bought a North Hollywood studio in 2000, 311 are currently about to release what is sure to be another hit record at the time of writing. Their career looks unassailable as long as the teenagers still enjoy their catchy mixture of hip-hop and rock – but as we've seen, anything can happen in this game. In the meantime, let them enjoy their success: after all, six years of climbing to the top would be too much for most of us. Let us hope they are enjoying it while it lasts.

TOOL

www.toolband.com

Metal fans tend to love or hate Tool: there are few in the middle ground. On the one hand, their take on modern metal is innovative, interesting, unpredictable and enjoyable. On the other, they seem to take themselves very seriously, irritating many because of their apparently arty progressive-rock leanings and often attracting ridicule for the antics of their frontman, who has been known to take to the stage in drag or clad only in skimpy underwear. Furthermore, the artistic and philosophical elements of Tool's work have led some critics to label them pretentious or plain self-indulgent. And of course, there are a thousand knob jokes to be made, just as there are with Helmet.

But however people perceive them, a mere handful of nu-metal bands are as prominent at the time of writing: the recipe is clearly working for someone. Broadly, Tool's music is dark, multifaceted and unusual: there are various obscure references to be found in their songs and the artwork of their releases, and understanding their message is easier if the listener is prepared to put in some

TOOL: Art attack

brainpower. They are, if you like, the thinking man's metal band.

Tool are old-school, in nu-metal terms. They first formed in 1990, and consisted for the next five years of Maynard James Keenan (vocals), Adam Jones (guitar), Paul D'Amour (bass) and Danny Carey (drums). In September 1995 D'Amour was replaced by ex-Peach four-stringer Justin Chancellor and the line-up has remained stable ever since.

The early band came together through one of the few other rap-metal bands in existence at the time – Rage Against The Machine, whose guitarist Tom Morello introduced his high-school friend Jones to Carey. Jones worked at the time in the film industry: one of his colleagues was D'Amour, and the band came together with the addition of Keenan, a friend of Morello's (he later sang guest vocals on 'Know Your Enemy', a standout track on RATM's self-titled debut album). Movie nerds will be interested to learn that Jones had worked on special effects for blockbusters such as *Jurassic Park* and the *Terminator* and *Predator* sequels: he can even be seen working on a dinosaur model in one scene of the *Making Of Jurassic Park* documentary.

The new band spent a year or so honing their impressive live act, fuelled by the powerful riffing of the three musicians and the often-mysterious lyrics of the obviously eccentric Keenan, who could boast a colourful past, including a three-

year spell in the US army. A deal was signed with the Volcano label, followed by an EP, *Opiate*, released in 1992. The recording gained Tool some immediate fans – its drug theme and philosophical ideas (the anaesthesia of the masses) were popular with the just-christened Generation X – but it was the first album, April 1993's *Undertow*, which saw Tool gather an identifiable fanbase. Like *Opiate*, the album had a message: its cover was a giant bar code (with all that such an image represents), and for a short time fans could request an alternative cover by writing to the address contained in the sleevenotes.

The first real exposure that the band received was on the Lollapalooza tour of 1993: they caused a sensation and the overwhelming crowd response led to their promotion from the second stage to the main stage during the tour. The next two years were spent building on this live foundation: many fans felt deprived of new material over this period, and it was with great expectation that a second album, *Aenima*, was released in October 1996. It was an immediate smash, and has since gone on to sell well over two million copies.

A very dark record, *Aenima*'s effect on Tool's fans was to cause them to close ranks around 'their' band: like Korn after them and Nirvana before them, Tool is a band with whom fans feel an intimate bond, perhaps due to the exclusivity they feel at being privy to the difficult-to-understand references mentioned above. This leads to a loyal fanbase, of course, and Tool continue to enjoy this privilege to this day.

The album was nominated for Best Recording Package at the 1997 Grammy Awards, but the fact that it didn't win was irrelevant to the fans, who were busy analysing the title, said to be an amalgam of 'anima', the ancient term for the human spirit, and 'enema'. An alternative theory suggests that it refers to a book, *Aegypt*, recommended by the band to their fans. A song, 'Aenema' (note spelling) did in fact win a Grammy for Best Metal Performance, and another nomination came up for 'Stinkfist' (which had had its lyrics altered by TV programmers for mainstream broadcasts) in the category of Best Music Video, Short Form.

Mystical themes that arose from the cover art of *Aenima* included Egyptian mythology (a seven-pointed star was depicted, which symbolises the goddess of love, Babalon) and the concept of 'sacred geometry', which states that the planet can be divided into mappable grids related to chromosomal patterns. Little wonder the fans were preoccupied...

1997 saw Tool touring further and falling into dispute with the Volcano label, which allegedly wanted the band to authorise the use of a song on the soundtrack of *Private Parts*, Howard Stern's semi-fictional autobiographical movie of that year. More serious problems arose when label and band embarked on legal action over contract renewal options: this was ultimately solved out of court the following year. However, management upsets and legal action followed, which are said to be ongoing.

Late 2000 saw the release of a live album, the punningly-titled *Salival*, which contained a full set of Tool crowd-pleasers, notably a cover of Led Zeppelin's 'No Quarter'. Tool have also been known to cover Kyuss' 'Demon Cleaner' and 'Stranglehold' by that red-blooded woodsman, Ted Nugent. The song 'You Lied' featured Buzz of the Melvins.

Although *Salival* was a popular release which sold well, there was a definite sense that a new studio album was in order (the gap between studio releases was now even longer than that between *Undertow* and *Aenima*) and so the arrival of *Lateralus* in May 2001 was very welcome. Named both after a human leg muscle (Tool have always harboured an ever-so-slightly macabre interest in body parts) and the

idea of thinking laterally, the album was supported by a strong single, 'Schism', whose creepy video got plenty of MTV airplay.

Tool's entry into the world of mainstream nu-metal appeared complete with the success of *Lateralus*, and further evidence of this could be seen in the plethora of extra-curricular activities in which the band – and especially Keenan – have been involved. The frontman's A Perfect Circle side-project was inescapable in its own right on the metal scene in 1999 and 2000, and a less serious band, Titannica, with Anthrax's Scott Ian and sometime Hole drummer Samantha Maloney,

TOOL: Maynard Jones Keenan – a man who clearly values his dignity

performed a song called 'Ass Kickin' Fat Kid' for the film *Run, Ronnie, Run.* Furthermore, Keenan recently co-wrote a song with one or more members of Nine Inch Nails for an as yet-incomplete album called *Tapeworm*, and appeared with Faith No More bassist Billy Gould and Rage Against The Machine's Morello and Brad Wilk on the Kiss tribute album *Kiss My Ass.* The line-up was known briefly as Shandi's Addiction. Finally, he also sang on the Deftones' Grammy-winning album *White Pony*.

The last word on the Tool phenomenon should be about that name. At first seeming like a harmless gag designed to get the establishment riled, it appears that the idea behind it is a fairly profound concept. Over the years the band have indicated that they believe in something called lachrymology, an unsubstantiated theory suggested by a pre-war writer called Ronald P. Vincent and based on the central tenet that the act of crying is therapeutic. Supposedly, the band wish to be identified as a 'tool' for helping people to understand lachrymology. Not convinced? Fair enough – as dedicated fans will attest, Tool have a habit of winding up their fans with sham theories, and this one may well be just another fine example of this tendency.

And so the band's story continues. Their fans love them obsessively; their enemies take every opportunity to slag them off as charlatans; and the rest of us look on in bewilderment. But one thing is for sure: jokers or not, Tool look set to get bigger and bigger (sorry, but the cheap gags are always the most irresistible).

TRIPSWITCH

www.tripswitch.co.uk

Based in the unlikely environs of rural Lincolnshire, Tripswitch consist of Jamie (vocals), Shaun (guitar), Rick (bass) and Pete (drums) and emerged from tiny hamlet communities to form one of Britain's newest nu-metal outfits. They're still in the process of finding a deal at the time of writing, but thanks to tours with noted metallers such as Raging Speedhorn, One Minute Silence, Tung, Brutal Deluxe, King Prawn and the unlikely Norwegian black metal band Immortal, plus a self-recorded EP, *Deleterious*, their profile is rising fast.

TWIZTID

www.twiztid.com

Sneered at by many observers as mere clones of the Insane Clown Posse, with whom Twiztid share a rather abrasive approach and certain carnival-esque themes, the duo of Jamie Madrox and the Monoxide Child sport the standard 'evil' make-up and knock out a relatively competent blend of rapping and riffing. 1998 saw the release of *Mostasteless*, while the follow-up effort, *Freek Show*, was issued on Halloween 2000.

What to say about this band? They look like the Insane Clown Posse. They *sound* like the Insane Clown Posse. So if you like the Insane Clown Posse, you'll probably like Twiztid. There comes a point when innovation is more important than image, and without being overly snide, it seems that Twiztid have stepped across that line.

ULTRASPANK

www.ultraspank.com

A prime example of a band who abandoned the old extreme metal template for pastures nu and took a giant step forward in the process, Ultraspank has its roots in a Californian speed metal outfit called Indica (hippies, eh?). This Santa Barbara-based band was adept enough to become MTV's Best College Rock Band of 1992, but was rapidly overtaken by the rising West Coast nu-metal scene, when the older, speedier template beat an unglamorous retreat to its Old World origins.

Indica's vocalist Pete Murray, bass player Dan Ogden and drummer Tyler Clark were too dedicated to simply fade away, however, and recruited Neil Godfrey (guitars/programming) and Jerry Oliviera (guitar). In 1995 they renamed the band Spank and started demoing more diverse material than the 'frash' of yore, rapidly gaining a set of fans on the Cali-metal scene.

The Epic label stepped forward with a deal in 1996 and a debut album was recorded, hindered only slightly by the band's obligation to change its name once more, this time to Ultraspank, having been alerted of a copyright issue.

The album, like so many others of this genre a self-titled work, was released in 1998 and the band backed it up with spots opening for Rob Zombie, Incubus, Sevendust, Soulfly, Korn and on the Ozzfest. Once the tours had finished, Ultraspank simply carried on playing: in the end it was estimated that they had toured North America a gruelling five times. Drummer Clark had had more then enough – well, can *you* imagine playing

UNION UNDERGROUND

www.unionunderground.com

Formed in San Antonio, Texas, Union Underground consisted initially of vocalist Bryan Scott and guitarist Patrick Kennison, who had been friends since their teenage years and who both graduated from high school in 1996. Embarking on a protracted studio recording schedule rather than studying for university degrees, the duo released a series of cassettes and distributed them by hand, eventually selling over 5,000 copies of an EP of industrial-flavoured metal.

UNION UNDERGROUND: Texan metallers

drums every night for that long? – and was replaced by James Carroll.

May 2000 saw the release of the second album, the aptly-titled *Progress*, which demonstrated that the band had moved on in style, while cocking a snook at the popular idea of scientific steps forward by featuring the famous mouse-with-human-ear on the cover. Since then Ultraspank have remained a festival fixture, although a much more successful release will be required if they are to avoid joining the mouse in the afterlife of a failed career.

This led to a deal with Portrait, a subsidiary of the Columbia empire, and a full band was soon in place after the signing-up of bassist John Moyer and drummer Josh Memelo in late 1998 and early 1999. Scott explained that he had signed his band to Columbia because he "didn't want to do the indie thing... it wouldn't have done us any justice". A full-length album, *An Education In Rebellion* (bless their little teenage hearts), was issued in 2000 and Union Underground have since gone on to play with several more established acts.

VEX RED

www.vexred.co.uk

It sounds like a joke, but it's true. How about this? Ross Robinson has a few months free in late 2000 before going into the studio to record Slipknot's second album, *Iowa*. He's looking for new bands to sign and produce. Speaking to *Kerrang!*, he states that any band who thinks they can match up should contact him via his record label. A short while later, he announces that a band has duly been found and signed up, having sent him a demo. And which band is it? A PVC-wearing, coke-snorting set of ex-models from Los Angeles? No. A masked troupe of goat-worshippers from Lonelyville, Idaho? No again: the lucky band to gain favour with the most pioneering producer in modern rock is a bunch of jeans-wearing teenagers from Aldershot in England. You couldn't make it up, could you?

Nick, Ant, Ben, Terry and Keith are Vex Red, the latest nu-metal band to come out of nowhere on this side of the Atlantic. Nick had sent in a CD in response to Robinson's request and forgotten all about it, when the phone rang one Sunday afternoon. At first assuming that some kind of prank was afoot, he was shaken when he finally realised that none other than the creator of *Korn*, *Slipknot* and *Three Dollar Bill, Y'All$* was on the line. After Ross had quizzed him about his band's lifestyles and ages, they agreed to meet next time Robinson was in the UK. A deal was signed via Ross' manager (who took Vex Red into his stable of acts) and the two parties met in July, 2000, at a rehearsal studio. Robinson brought Casey Chaos of Amen along to hear Vex Red play the music they themselves describe as 'controlled noise', although Chaos' presence made the young band hit the odd wrong note here and there.

The band were hindered somewhat by the departure of their drummer a couple of weeks before Ross' appearance, but recruited a friend to the drum-stool with time to spare, and the sessions duly went ahead in Cornwall, the location having been chosen both for its distance from their home town and the relaxing ambience of the area. When the time came to record the album, Robinson applied his tried-and-tested studio techniques of working the band up into a frenzy: vocalist Terry recorded his vocals from inside a tiny wardrobe-sized booth known as The Rocks, with no lighting or ventilation. Well, it worked for Corey Taylor, Jonathan Davis and the aforementioned Chaos, after all.

At the time of writing, only a Vex Red demo has been released to the press – bizarrely, in MP3 format, distributed on floppy disks. However, expectations are building for the 'new Ross Robinson band': let us hope that this does not prove to be too heavy a millstone for the band to bear.

VIDEODRONE

www.videodrone.com

Like Orgy, Videdrone are a versatile, electronic-sounding metal band with plenty of charisma and PVC stage costumes, and were signed by Korn to their Elementree label in the late Nineties. Unlike Orgy, however, Videodrone have a surprising amount of history behind them, having formed as long ago as 1988 and releasing a handful of albums before Korn was even thought of.

Singer Ty Elam, guitarist David File, bassist Mavis, keyboard player Rohan and drummer Kris Kohls first played together as the very black metal-sounding Cradle Of Thorns, a Bakersfield, California-based band that would often travel the desert journey to LA to play there. The band later moved to the Huntingdon Beach area and signed to the Triple X label (also home to Jane's Addiction and Social Distortion) before releasing a series of albums from 1990, including *Remember It Day*, *Feed Us* and the popular *Download This*, which included a cover of Mötley Crüe's 'Shout At The Devil'. Shows with Sunny Day Real Estate, Sugar Ray and the Offspring saw a local fanbase gather.

In the meantime, their friends and Bakersfield brethren Korn had gone stratospheric in 1994 with their self-titled debut album, and offered their old pals a deal on their new label as well as giving them the support slot on a tour. In the interim Cradle Of Thorns had marked this change in fortunes by changing its name to Videodrone (a moniker adapted from the sci-fi B-movie, *Videodrome*).

A self-titled album followed, featuring the talents of Korn singer Jonathan Davis and Limp Bizkit's Fred Durst, and was produced by Korn bassist Fieldy. Tours with Rob Zombie and, yes, Korn kept sales healthy and, let's face it, Videodrone look set for life.

VISION OF DISORDER

www.vod.com

Like their fellow New Yorkers Biohazard, Vision Of Disorder honed an act based on uncompromising hardcore punk and thrash metal and became one of the city's most popular underground bands in a short space of time. Formed on Long Island in 1992, and consisting of vocalist Tim Williams, guitarists Matt Baumbach and Mike Kennedy, bassist Mike Fleischmann and drummer Brendon Cohen, the band played solidly for three long years before the compilers of the now-seminal *New York's Hardest* collection approached them with a request for a track. This was followed by an EP, *Still*, released on the band's own Striving For Togetherness label, which brought Vision Of Disorder to the attention of Roadrunner.

An eponymous debut followed and, although it was a moderate success, the band seemed dissatisfied with it. Fleischmann actually departed for a college career: undaunted, VOD simply carried on without bothering to recruit a replacement four-stringer, and he returned to the fold after a few months of absence.

Tours with Machine Head and on the inaugural Ozzfest in 1997 saw the band attract a devoted audience. The mood in the camp was much improved, it seemed, when the time came for another album, and *Imprint* was a much more melodic, professionally-crafted effort. Recorded in a mere nineteen days, the ferocity of the music was impressive, as was a guest appearance by Pantera's Philip Anselmo, recorded on his home turf of New Orleans.

Since then, two more albums, 1999's *For Bleeders* and 2001's *From Bliss to Devastation* (the latter released after a move to the TVT

VISION OF DISORDER: Long Island hardcore

label) has seen VOD remain a much-praised live and studio act, although a jump to stadium level seems improbable at this stage. However, there's always room in the lower levels of metallic activity for a committed hardcore band, and Vision Of Disorder seem to be in it for the long haul.

WILL HAVEN

www.willhaven.com

Stuck for a name and settling on that of a fictitious character, William Haven, this Sacramento four-piece formed in 1995 and consists of permanent members Grady Avenell (vocals), Jeff Irwin (guitar) and Michael Martin (bass). The original drummer was Wayne Morse, later replaced by Dave Hulse, who in turn yielded the drum stool to Mitch Wheeler.

The band released a 7-track self-titled EP the following year, of which thousands of copies were rapidly sold via mail-order and at West Coast gigs opening for bands of the calibre of Beastie Boys and Earth Crisis. The Revelation label signed them up after a significant fanbase had assembled and, in April 1997, sessions commenced for a full-length album.

The result, the remarkably heavy *El Diablo*, found high-profile fans such as Max Cavalera of Soulfly and Chino Moreno of Deftones publicly singing its praises, and hit the top spot on several local charts. An American tour with the latter act and Limp Bizkit followed, as well as an East Coast jaunt with Big Apple hardcore-mongers Vision Of Disorder and a Deftones support slot in Europe.

The follow-up, 1999's Andy Sneap-produced *WHVN*, appeared just as a tour with Slipknot was arranged: the Iowan nine-piece had just released their self-titled album to enormous acclaim and were hitting as many cities as they could manage while the initial shock lasted. The Havens were delighted to go along for the ride, as were the openers Kittie.

Avenell put in a memorable vocal cameo on Soulfly's *Primitive* album (he, the Fly's Max Cavalera and Moreno swapped throat-shredding vocals on 'Pain'). Before he and the band retired to the studio once again for a third album, *Carpe Diem*, which is scheduled for release in late 2001.

WORKHORSE MOVEMENT

www.workhorsemovement.com

A potent rap-metal band formed by four students sick of the predictable college lifestyle, Workhorse Movement was first mooted during the week of Woodstock 94 by Central Michigan University chemistry student and singer Matt Kozuch-Rea (who goes by the name Myron on stage). Together with guitarist Jeff Piper, bassist Jay and drummer Joe Mackie, Myron worked up a hardcore set and the band began to attract followers, initially around their Mount Pleasant campus (at student parties – sounds a bit like *Porky's*, eh?) but later throughout the entire state of Michigan.

After a year of touring, WM recorded an album, *Dopamine*, and released it to some local acclaim. While the record did well enough to keep the band's spirits high, they recognised that their location wasn't doing

them any favours and relocated to Detroit, where the Overcore label offered them a contract. A self-titled EP was subsequently issued and the gruelling live schedule was resumed.

Tours with a plethora of bands of all stripes followed, including Skinlab, Sevendust, Gravity Kills and, er, Vanilla Ice (who is said at the time of writing to be writing metal tunes). Bassist Jay returned to university and was replaced by ex-20 Dead Flower Children player Jeff Wright, while a second vocalist, Chris Sparks (aka Cornbread) was also recruited.

Things took a different turn when Roadrunner expressed an interest in signing the Workhorses, and a contract was negotiated after the departure of Grady (the old revolving-door syndrome again), whose place was filled by Pete Bever. The Roadrunner debut, 2000's very Western-titled *Sons Of The Pioneers*, saw new fans gravitate towards the Movement in droves, and solid festival and club appearances kept the Horses galloping onward.

However, dspite all appearances to the contrary, things weren't working out within the WH camp, and in early 2001 the band abruptly split with little or no explanation. Your guess is as good as mine, although the band hinted to *Terrorizer* magazine that financial stresses lay behind the split. The root of all evil, eh?

ZAPRUDER

www.zapruder.co.uk

Named after the amateur cameraman who filmed the assassination of John F. Kennedy in 1963, Edinburgh's Zapruder – consisting of Roland, Keith and Scott – are a punk/nu-metal band with one album to their names, 2000's *Obsessive/Compulsive*, recorded on a four-track machine and released by the band themselves. Scotland's metal scene is confined largely to the city clubs, where Zapruder are making a name for themselves, and which are probably the best place to see this aggressive young band before larger venues lessen their live impact.

ZAPRUDER: Still in the underground

ZEBRAHEAD

www.nutsen.com/zebrahead/index.html

Mixing punk, rap-metal and Blink 182-like juvenilia (notably a penchant for surgically-enhanced models), Zebrahead were formed in 1996 by singer Justin Mauriello, guitarist Greg Bergdorf, bassist Ben Osmundson and the unpronounceably-christened drummer Ed Udhus. Playing live in the epicentre of Nineties punk – Orange County, California, home to shouty types such as the Offspring – the constant doses of gob-tastic ska-punkishness led to some disillusionment with the whole genre among the Zebrahead ranks, who actively pushed their music towards hip-hop by recruiting a rapper, Ali Tabatabaee.

Attracted by their powerful performances, the Dr. Dream label approached the band and the *Yellow* EP was released in May 1998. This led to a contract with Columbia (a considerable step upwards), for whom Zebrahead recorded an album, *Waste Of Mind*, notable for its inventive riffing and the presence of porn star Ron Jeremy. The record also received a Grammy nomination for Best Metal Performance.

Taking the 'parrot-choking' theme to another level, the next album, August 2000's *Playmate Of The Year* featured the *Playboy* model Jodi Ann Patterson on its cover, while the title track became a successful single largely due to the video which accompanied it, which included a cameo by none other than Hugh Hefner himself. Standout tracks on *POTY* included Lit singer AJ Popoff on 'What's Goin' On' and the Ricky Martin piss-take of 'Livin' Libido Loco'.

And on they go. Nu-metal: who says it's just for boys?

ZERO CIPHER

www.zerocipher.com

Still unsigned at the time of publication, Zero Cipher have been hailed as among the most exciting proponents among the few British nu-metal bands. Combining the expected turntablism with hardcore song structures and meaty downtuned guitar riffs, the band have already been compared to Raging Speedhorn, despite only having released a hard-to-find three-track demo to date.

The band, about whom details are sketchy, are a six-piece and come from the south of England, where they were formed in 1998. The 'zero cipher' is a concept extracted from a variety of ancient texts and seems to have been well-chosen to represent their dark, sometimes impenetrable sound. Having recovered from a seemingly incessant bout of personnel changes, they have secured opening slots with near-underground bands such as Breakneck, Snub and Vacant Stare. A debut album is said to be scheduled for release in 2001, so keep your eye on those club listings before Zero Cipher make good on their early promise – and are hauled off to the Ozzfest...

MOVERS & SHAKERS

THE MOST INFLUENTIAL PEOPLE AND ORGANISATIONS IN NU-METAL, AND WHERE TO FIND THEM IN THIS BOOK

BIAFRA, JELLO (musician/label chief)
Nailbomb, Segression, Sepultura

CAVALERA, MAX (musician)
Fear Factory, Fudge Tunnel, Ill Nino, Nailbomb, Snot, Soulfly, Will Haven

CAZARES, DINO (musician)
Coal Chamber, Fear Factory, Nailbomb, Soulfly, Spineshank

CRAHAN, SHAWN (musician)
Mudvayne, Slipknot

DATE, TERRY (producer)
Deftones, Limp Bizkit, Staind

DJ LETHAL (musician)
Limp Bizkit, Professional Murder Music, Soulfly, Staind

DURST, FRED (musician, producer)
Cold, Korn, Limp Bizkit, Methods Of Mayhem, Primus, Puddle Of Mudd, Rage Against The Machine, Soulfly, Staind, Taproot, Videodrone

FAMILY VALUES (tour)
Incubus, Korn, Limp Bizkit, Orgy, Puddle Of Mudd, Rammstein

JORDISON, JOEY (musician)
Marilyn Manson, Slipknot

KORN (band)
Downer, Hed (Pe), Human Waste Project, Incubus, Life Of Agony, Limp Bizkit, Orgy, Pitchshifter, Rammstein, Rorschach Test, Soulfly, Static-X, Ultraspank, Videodrone

MANSON, MARILYN (musician)
Godhead, Slipknot

MORENO, CHINO (musician)
Autonomy, Deftones, Sevendust, Soulfly, Will Haven

OZZFEST (annual festival)
Apartment 26, Disturbed, Drowning Pool, Earth Crisis, Godsmack, Hed (Pe), Incubus, Limp Bizkit, Minus 313, Raging Speedhorn, Sevendust, Shuvel, Slaves On Dope, Soulfly, System Of A Down, Taproot, Ultraspank, Vision Of Disorder

RICHARDSON, COLIN (producer)
One Minute Silence, Pulkas

RICHARDSON, GARTH 'GGGARTH' (producer)
40 Below Summer, Kittie, Mudvayne, Nickelback, Snot, Spineshank

ROADRUNNER (record label)
Amen, Biohazard, Keith Caputo, Coal Chamber, Crease, Dog Eat Dog, Downer, Dry Kill Logic, Earth Crisis, Fear Factory, Ill Nino, Nickelback, Slipknot, Soulfly, Spineshank, Vision Of Disorder, Workhorse Movement

ROBINSON, ROSS (producer)
Amen, At The Drive-In, Coal Chamber, Glassjaw, Human Waste Project, Limp Bizkit, Slipknot, Soulfly, Vex Red

ONLINE RESOURCES

The internet is invaluable for the curious metaller, which is
why I've provided a web address for each of the bands in this book.
But for more general information, try these websites:

www.liquidmetalradio.cjb.net
www.metalhammer.co.uk
www.nu-metal.co.uk
www.fubarm.com
www.tyler.demon.co.uk/metalweb
www.hardradio.com
www.knac.com
www.roadrun.com
www.rollingstone.com
www.sonicnet.com